# WORKING ON CONTRACT
# WORLDWIDE

From Vanda,
7th sept '01.

# Other How To Books on Living & Working Abroad

Applying for a United States Visa
Finding a Job in Canada
Finding Work Overseas
Become an Au Pair
Do Voluntary Work Abroad
Emigrate
Find Temporary Work Abroad
Get a Job Abroad
Get a Job in America
Get a Job in Australia
Get a Job in Europe
Get a Job in France
Get a Job in Germany
Get a Job in Hotels & Catering
Get a Job in Travel & Tourism
Live & Work in America
Live & Work in Australia
Live & Work in France
Live & Work in Germany
Live & Work in the Gulf
Live & Work in Hong Kong
Live & Work in Italy
Live & Work in Japan
Live & Work in New Zealand

Live & Work in Portugal
Live & Work in Saudia Arabia
Live & Work in Spain
Living & Working in Britain
Living & Working in Canada
Living & Working in China
Living & Working in the Netherlands
Master Languages
Obtaining Visas & Work Permits
Rent & Buy Property in France
Rent & Buy Property in Italy
Retire Abroad
Selling into Japan
Setting Up Home in Florida
Spend a Year Abroad
Study Abroad
Teach Abroad
Travel Round the World
Working Abroad
Working in Japan
Working in the Gulf
Woring on Contract Worldwide
Your Own Business in Europe

*Other titles in preparation*

The How To series now contains more than 150 titles
in the following categories:

Business Basics
Family Reference
Jobs & Careers
Living & Working Abroad
Student Handbooks
Successful Writing

Please send for a free copy of the latest catalogue for full details
(see back cover for address)

LIVING & WORKING ABROAD

# WORKING ON
# CONTRACT
# WORLDWIDE

How to triple your earnings by working
as an independent contractor anywhere
in the world

## Rod Briggs

How To Books

**British Library Cataloguing-in-Publication data**
A catalogue record for this book is available from the British Library.

© Copyright 1996 by Rodney V. Briggs.

First published in 1996 by How To Books Ltd, Plymbridge House, Estover Road, Plymouth PL6 7PZ, United Kingdom.

*Note:* The material contained in this book is set out in good faith for general guidance and no liability can be accepted for loss or expense incurred as a result of relying in particular circumstances on statements made in the book. The laws and regulations are complex and liable to change, and readers should check the current position with the relevant authorities before making personal arrangements.

Produced for How To Books by Deer Park Productions.
Typeset by Kestrel Data, Exeter.
Printed and bound in Great Britain by
Cromwell Press, Broughton Gifford, Melksham, Wilts.

# Contents

# List of Illustrations

# Preface

This book is about money and how almost anybody in a white collar, engineering related discipline (or other profession) can make a great deal of it, at least doubling, possibly trebling and maybe even quadrupling his income. All he has to do is to give up permanent staff employment and become a contractor.

Contractors are paid far more than permanent staff employees because they are prepared to accept short-term employment, the risk of long-term unemployment and the inconvenience of working away from home and often abroad.

Contracting is untried by most people and consequently something of a mystery, surrounded by strange tales and mis-understandings. Myth number one would have you believe that you need extraordinary professional and personal qualities to be a contractor, that only those possessing exceptional abilities can command the vast incomes that contractors are known to earn, let alone cope with working abroad.

This is totally untrue. The average contractor is no better qualified, professionally or personally, than his contemporary in permanent employment. The only person who is not suitable to be a contractor is he who cannot make up his mind to become one or who is no good at his permanent job. Even age is not a criterion. It is not unusual to find contractors in their sixties.

There is no magic formula involved in becoming a contractor. Anyone can do it. Contractors are made, not born. All you need are professional competence, the will to succeed and a little information.

Until now one of the biggest problems in entering contracting has been in finding out what it was all about. Many is the contractor who has said, 'I wish I'd known about this years ago'.

The subject has been mysterious partly because of its lack of specialised literature. With no handbook or other guidance, it has usually been necessary to become a contractor in order to find out what contracting is all about.

The would-be contractor, aware perhaps of the existence of contracting and its financial advantages but having no work of reference devoted to the subject, has had to rely on hearsay for information and advice. With only this vague guidance available, many have been reluctant to sacrifice the so-called security of permanent employment for the unknown quantities of contracting.

Others, more adventurous perhaps, have blundered into contracting unprepared. Some have prospered for all their lack of preparation. Some have come seriously to grief. There is far more to successful contracting than signing your first contract.

Contracting is a business and like any other it can be learned—as long as you have the information. This book will provide that information and by so doing also clear away the mysteries that surround the subject and place its problems in their proper perspective.

The most difficult part of becoming a contractor is making up your mind to become one. This book will not do that for you. It will, however, explain how to become a contractor, how to cope with the professional, commercial and personal aspects of contracting and how to make the best of the opportunities that contracting can offer.

The book will also give you an idea of what to expect when you go on contract. Contracting is not just a matter of going to work somewhere else under slightly different circumstances from those you are used to. It is a way of life with its own set of rules.

The book is arranged to take the aspiring contractor through the business from the enquiry stage onwards. Reference to the Contents pages will locate whichever topic interests you.

Although emphasis is given to the pitfalls that await the unwary, it is not intended to expand the myth that contracting is fraught with unavoidable ambushes. Contracting has its ups and downs like any other activity. Most of the dangers mentioned in this book are potential rather inevitable. If you hear of a ghastly mishap that has befallen some unlucky contractor in the past, it does not follow that the same thing is bound to happen to you.

Whatever your discipline, there is a contract somewhere that would benefit from your skills. As long as you have the confidence to sell your abilities, there is no reason why you should not succeed as a contractor. If you are careful you will also benefit from the high earnings that contracting will bring you.

As a contractor you will move fairly frequently, either within the UK or abroad and will accumulate experience of work, places, people and things at a vastly accelerated rate compared to the man who remains static in one job. Contracting is rewarding, stimulating and mind expanding. It can become addictive.

Readers are recommended to seek professional advice before making important business, legal or financial decisions, and this book should not be considered a substitute for such advice.

Thanks are given to all those who have assisted in the preparation of this book, especially:

- The Institute of Chartered Accountants
- Bridges & Holland, chartered accountants
- Mr D. Mason of DBM Technical Services (London) Ltd,
- Mr I. Maturin of Technical Aid International Inc.

and to all those contractors who have allowed their experiences to be drawn upon, not least Mr Paul Smith and Mr Alan Hedges.

*Rodney V. Briggs*

# 1
# When it's Time for a Change

This chapter deals with the following:

- first thoughts about contracting
- what a contractor actually is
- who uses contractors and why
- assessing the risks
- contract locations
- contracting in the UK and abroad
- contract agents

## First thoughts

Picture a scene. You are at work. You are a permanent staff employee of an engineering company in one of the white collar disciplines. You could be anything from a technical clerk to a design engineer. You are paid a fair salary for your services. You work a set number of hours per week and have an agreed annual leave. You have occasional overtime and one day you may be promoted. You might be content with your lot or wish you could make a change and find some way to make a great deal more money.

Most people seeking to move look for another staff job which will at least provide a change of scene. They normally scan the newspapers Sits. Vac. and if they even notice the small ads. often dismiss them as they are for mysterious people called contractors who work in a twilight, freelance world beyond the ken of normal folk and therefore not worth bothering about.

You may think the same but before you read on you might pause to wonder what contracting really is and whether it would be suitable for you.

## WHAT IS A CONTRACTOR?

'Contractor: One who enters into a contract to supply a product or provide a service.'
*From Defence Standard 00-40 (Part 1)/Issue 2 (ARMP-1)*

In the context of this book a contractor is an individual with a marketable skill who is hired by an agency to provide a temporary, specialised service to a client company in the UK or abroad.

### Why use contractors?

Many companies use contractors at the commencement of new projects. This may be because they do not have adequate staff or in-house expertise to meet the new contingency, or because the company is unwilling to commit itself to recruiting permanent staff, with all its legal obligations to them, at a stage before a project has proved itself viable.

Contractors offer companies flexibility. When a requirement arises a contractor may be hired for a limited period much more readily than a staff employee.

The contractor works according to the conditions of a contract agreed between himself and the agency. The agent has his own contract with the client. The agent charges the client for the contractor's services, deducts about 15 per cent for himself and passes the remainder to the contractor on a weekly or monthly basis. The contractor is usually paid by the hour but occasionally by the day (see Signing a Contract in Chapter 2).

### Who isn't a contractor?

It is worth noting that the contractor's form of hourly payment distinguishes his from other forms of temporary employment, and that plenty of people besides contractors work abroad. These latter may be staff employees seconded overseas by their usual employer or they may take employment abroad for a specified period. If an agent is involved at all he will usually take a one-off recruitment fee rather than an ongoing percentage. Salaries are quoted by the calendar duration of the job, e.g. annually, and often form part of an all-in package that includes relocation, paid leave, housing, schooling, medical care and transport. Such conditions are often found in the oil fields and construction industries in developing countries, especially in the Middle East, whose very infrastructure means that western style facilities, notably accommodation, are unavailable locally and must be provided by the employing company in the form of expatriate camps and compounds independent of the host community. Employees are commonly known as 'expats'.

The true contractor has no all-in remuneration package, no paid leave and no assistance with accommodation. His agent and the client have no obligations to him other than to pay him his hourly rate. The contractor receives the whole of his income as cash (minus deductions for tax and social security where applicable) rather than partly in services. His leaves are not specified and his absence from work is by mutual agreement with the client. The contractor stands on his own two feet and looks after his own needs.

It is uncommon, although not unheard of, for contractors to become expats and vice versa. Few agents deal with both categories, both employer and employed preferring to operate in their own particular spheres.

## Question and answer session

Q. *Are contractors cheaper or more expensive to industry than permanent staff?*

A. This question is a hoary old apple and the answer varies according to point of view and vested interest. Contractors and their agents will tell you that contractors are cheaper while trades unions and their members in staff employment will disagree. On balance though, contractors are generally cheaper.

Q. *Then, if contractors are so useful and cheaper too, why doesn't industry use nothing else?*

A. Firstly, because there simply aren't enough contractors to go round and secondly, because companies need to maintain a stable hard core of in-house expertise. Some companies may use contractors only occasionally while others have a permanent, high proportion of contractors in their labour force.

Q. *It has been rumoured that my employer is going to place all its staff on one year, renewable contracts. Will this make me a contractor?*

A. Not really. You will be signing a contract of employment, not a contract to supply services. Although this is becoming more common, it will not give you the benefit of a true contractor's rate of pay.

## HOW MUCH DO CONTRACTORS EARN?

Unfortunately it is not possible to provide a meaningful table of contract rates as they vary enormously according to;

- discipline
- industry
- client company
- location
- supply and demand

The variation can be as much as 60 per cent for a given discipline within one industry for a UK contract.

As a very rough rule of thumb however, you should expect as a minimum to double your gross income for UK contracts. For foreign assignments you should at least double and possibly treble your gross income. With probable tax advantages abroad, the increase in your net income will be proportionately much higher (see Tax and Social Security and Applying the One Sixth Rule in Chapter 3).

## ISN'T CONTRACTING RISKY?

There is an element of risk in almost every human activity and contracting is no exception. But are the risks of going contracting, especially that of long unemployment between contracts, really any greater than in staying in permanent employment, particularly when contracting's greater rewards are taken into account?

### Quantifying the risk
The very word 'permanent' is a misnomer where employment is concerned. 'Not temporary' would be a better description, if only because the terms of engagement have no cut-off date. To the staff employee, that means security. But even permanent employment has an element of risk; you can be fired or much more likely in today's world, made redundant. Alternative staff positions can be

more difficult to find than contracts and staff salaries do not provide much scope for saving against a rainy day.

A contractor, conversely, is hired for a limited period; the end of his employment is visible. Most contracts however, either contain provision for extension or are extended. The sensible contractor minimises the risk of unemployment and uses his high rate of pay to ensure that if he does have a period of idleness, it is not a disaster.

## Minimising the risk

The first time contractor should seek contracts offering a high probability of one year's employment. A year on contract, especially on continental rates with attendant tax advantages, can provide a very healthy financial cushion should he need it. Additionally:

- follow several contract leads at a time because the one that seems to be certain is probably the one that will fail to materialise

- keep yourself abreast of current requirements even when you are employed

- keep in touch with agents

- be organised and don't trust to luck.

## Question and answer session

Q. *If I leave my staff position to go contracting, will my former employer take me back if anything goes wrong?*

A. Probably not, even if you could eat humble pie and ask to go back.

Q. *Could I become a contractor with my present employer?*

A. Most unlikely. This is not an option to finding a contract out in the big, wide world.

Q. *Is there any long-term possibility of ever coming back to my present employer as a contractor, if for example I want to live at home and remain a contractor?*

A. This is not unheard of, although a 'decent' span of time is usually required to elapse between departure and return, usually to mute the inevitable jealousy of your former colleagues.

Q. *I'm very interested in becoming a contractor but I'm worried about what happens when my first contract ends. Will I earn a lot of money for a period and then nothing at all when I'm out of work for ages afterwards?*

A. Every aspiring contractor has these concerns. The length of time that it takes you to find a first contract may guide you as to your marketability. Remember that the longer you remain a contractor, accumulating wealth and perhaps developing alternative income from investments, the less it will matter whether you find an immediate continuation contract or not.

## WHICH INDUSTRIES USE CONTRACTORS AND WHERE ARE THEY?

### The industries

Possibilities for contract employment exist wherever industry is to be found, whether in the UK or overseas. In most cases the industry will be in the equipment manufacturing sector but some process industries will be found. The majority of contract openings lie within the aerospace/defence industries where British contractors are always in demand if only because English is the working international language of this sector.

The following industries are the main users of contractors worldwide:

| | |
|---|---|
| Aerospace | Defence |
| Petro-chemical | Automotive |
| Railway | Communications |
| Agriculture | Medical |
| Optical | Machine tool |
| Mining | Computer hardware & software |
| Mechanical handling | Power generation |
| Construction | Ship building |
| Nuclear | Public utilities |
| Process control | Domestic appliance |
| Electronics | Information technology |

## The locations
As in the past and for the foreseeable future, the majority of contract openings that you see advertised will be for the UK and Europe. Many contractors in fact, never work outside the UK, preferring either to remain within weekend commuting distance of home or finding sufficient work to keep them occupied without the need to go abroad. Where overseas contracting is mentioned in this book, it is with Europe mostly in mind.

## Europe
Germany with its huge industrial base has traditionally absorbed more British contractors than any other continental country. At the time of writing though, a combination of world recession and the strains of unification have meant that contracts in Germany have been difficult to find of late. How long this situation will continue is difficult to say.

After Germany, the Netherlands with its aircraft and electronics industries, is a popular country for contractors. Opportunities also exist in France, Italy and Spain and to a lesser extent in Belgium and Luxembourg.

Switzerland and Austria present possibilities although Swiss industry is constrained in the recruitment of non-Swiss nationals by work permit restrictions. Permits in any case tend to be short term and their renewal can be difficult. Sweden also absorbs some contractors in its aircraft industry although the likelihood of high taxation deters many.

## Further afield
Beyond Europe, North America takes quite a few contractors while Australia and Israel have some opportunities. South Africa has traditionally been a difficult area because of its political situation although a number of contractors have worked there. With political settlement now in sight, this country has the potential to be one of the great contract venues in the near future. Work is also to be found in Taiwan and Indonesia, mostly in aerospace. There are occasionally contract openings in Hong Kong and other countries of the Pacific rim.

## The future
Looking ahead, it is in the newly free countries of Eastern Europe that the greatest potential lies. The need to modernise outmoded plant and equipment in order to compete in the new market

economy will require western expertise, although it is too early to say at what pace events will develop and what the eventual demand for contractors may be.

## INTRODUCING THE CONTRACT AGENT

More maligned than praised, the agent is an indispensable part of the contract business. Without him, the whole system would collapse. A good agent is worth his weight in gold.

> *Note:* 'Agent' and 'agency' are both used in this book. Strictly speaking, the agent is an individual working within an agency.

The term 'agent' is generic and loosely covers a variety of organisations that supply contract staff to industry. The majority of agencies are very small, employing two or three staff and operating from a single office. Others are much larger and sometimes eschew the very word 'agency', preferring to style themselves 'recruitment consultants' or 'consulting engineers'. As you will discover, size and efficiency are quite unrelated.

### Why use an agent?
The agent exists in order to match many different skills with a vast range of needs. With his database of contractors and his detailed knowledge of many client companies and their requirements for temporary staff with special abilities, the agent is a facilitator for both parties, saving each the time consuming bother of dealing with the other on an individual basis.

### Dealing with agents
When you are looking for a contract you will probably be dealing with a fair number of agents simultaneously. You will almost certainly find the experience frustrating. This is due more to the nature of contracting than to shortcomings on the part of agents.

### The things that will frustrate you
- You telephone an agent on spec and find that you can neither get any sense out of the girl who answers the phone nor will she connect you with anyone else but simply tells you to send in your CV.

- You get through to the person you want to speak to and get the same reaction as above.

- You call about an advertised vacancy and still get the same reaction.

- The agent calls you about a vacancy, asks if you are free and interested but won't give you any information.

- You follow a lead for a contract and go through all the stages including an interview, are accepted for the job and then hear nothing more. When you call the agent to find out what might be happening, you find yourself again unable to get past the uncommunicative telephonist.

- You endure months of silence and have probably written the whole episode off to experience, when the agent phones out of the blue and asks if you can start work next Monday.

## The Deafening Silence

The Deafening Silence is one of the annoyances of contracting that you will soon learn to live with. Agents should, for example, at least acknowledge receipt of your CV. Many do, but plenty don't.

However irritating this lack of communication may be, it isn't always due to stupidity, awkwardness, bad manners or inefficiency but rather to commercial secrecy. Agents are in fierce competition with each other. When the girl at the other end of the phone seems loathe to speak to you, she has probably been told to give nothing away. The alleged applicant might actually be a rival agent trying to find out if there is a juicy new contract in the offing that he doesn't know about. The fear is real; agents have gone out of business through careless talk.

If you think an agent is messing you about, remember that he may have problems too. Equipment end users and government departments are indecisive in placing orders which adversely affects a manufacturer's ability to state his requirement for contract staff, thus leaving the agent in a difficult situation with recruiting.

## Case history: learning to live with the patter

As a newcomer to contracting, Dennie Bright quickly developed the near contempt for agents expressed by some of his colleagues. Agents, he decided, would seldom bother to talk to you unless you could fill a vacancy for them. If you could, they would resort to any amount of persuasive waffle to get you on site and earning a commission for them, however personally unsuitable regarding rate or location the job might be for you. Agents he believed, were little better than time-share salesmen.

Later, Dennis came to appreciate that selling was part of an agent's job, and that the agent who could sell an assignment to a contractor could also sell a contractor to a client.

## Cowboy agents

Infinitely worse than the agent who inadvertently annoys you is the real cowboy, the sharp operator who sets up dodgy deals and rips off his own contract staff. They pop up during booms but tend to fade during recessions.

Most cowboys are small time operators, often people who have worked with a reputable agency and have set up on their own using information they have accumulated or even stolen.

Some are large, outwardly respectable and survive for years, often by bribery of individuals within client companies.

Favourite cowboy tricks include:

- Weasel worded contracts.

- Late payment.

- Non-payment.

- Part payment.

- Fiddled exchange rates.

- Defaulting on end-of-contract payments.

- Defaulting on payment for time saved by contractors on fixed price contracts.

- Calculatedly complex time sheets and payslips designed to confuse the contractor who thinks he is being short changed.

- Blaming the banking system for interruptions to the money flow.

- Blaming their own accounts department for shortfalls in payment, when said department often consists solely of the agent's wife.

If you are owed money by a cowboy, go to your solicitor. He will tell you whether you have a chance of making a successful claim and if its likely costs will outweigh the gains. If the agent has gone out of business you may have to write the whole thing off to experience.

Better still is to avoid cowboys in the first place. Your best protection, until other contractors warn you who to avoid, is to be guided by your instincts. Listen to the chat that you hear over the phone and see if it rings true. If you meet the agent face-to-face in the initial stages you will have a good opportunity to form an opinion of him. If you get as far as signing a contract, your solicitor should spot any hidden catches in its wording. If your suspicions are aroused, leave well alone.

However depressing the foregoing may seem, your chances of meeting an outright cowboy are very remote. The majority of agents are honest and will do their best for their contract staff and ensure that all monies are paid on time. Agents after all, have a vested interest in keeping their contractors happy.

## Question and answer session

Q. *If I phone an agent on spec and he won't tell me anything except to send in my CV, what should I do?*

A. Submit your CV anyway. If the agent can't be bothered to talk to you it's probably because your chances of his getting a contract for you are slim, at least at present, but they will be slimmer still if he does not have your details on file for the future.

Q. *If receipt of my CV is not acknowledged, should I worry?*

A. No, not unless you were responding to a definite requirement, in which case you should at least elicit a verbal confirmation that your CV has arrived.

Q. *Is there any way in which a cowboy agent will give himself away?*

A. Yes. If he asks you for a registration fee, don't have any more to do with him.

# 2
# Becoming a Contractor

Once you have made up your mind that you would like to become a contractor, the problem remains of how to go about it. The mere act of signing your first contract makes you a contractor in name only. The actual process of becoming a contractor, of growing out of the mental habits of permanent staff employment, of learning the business of contracting and above all, of learning to think like a contractor takes rather longer.

Anyone can become a contractor. All contractors were staff employees once. All you need is information. This chapter deals with the following:

- how to get into contracting
- preparing your approach
- looking for contracts
- finding an accountant
- interviews
- dealing with agents
- contract duration
- signing a contract
- work permits

## Taking the first steps
Before you even begin to look for contracts, you must:

- prepare a CV

- establish a contact book

- make sure that you have a valid passport if you hope to work abroad.

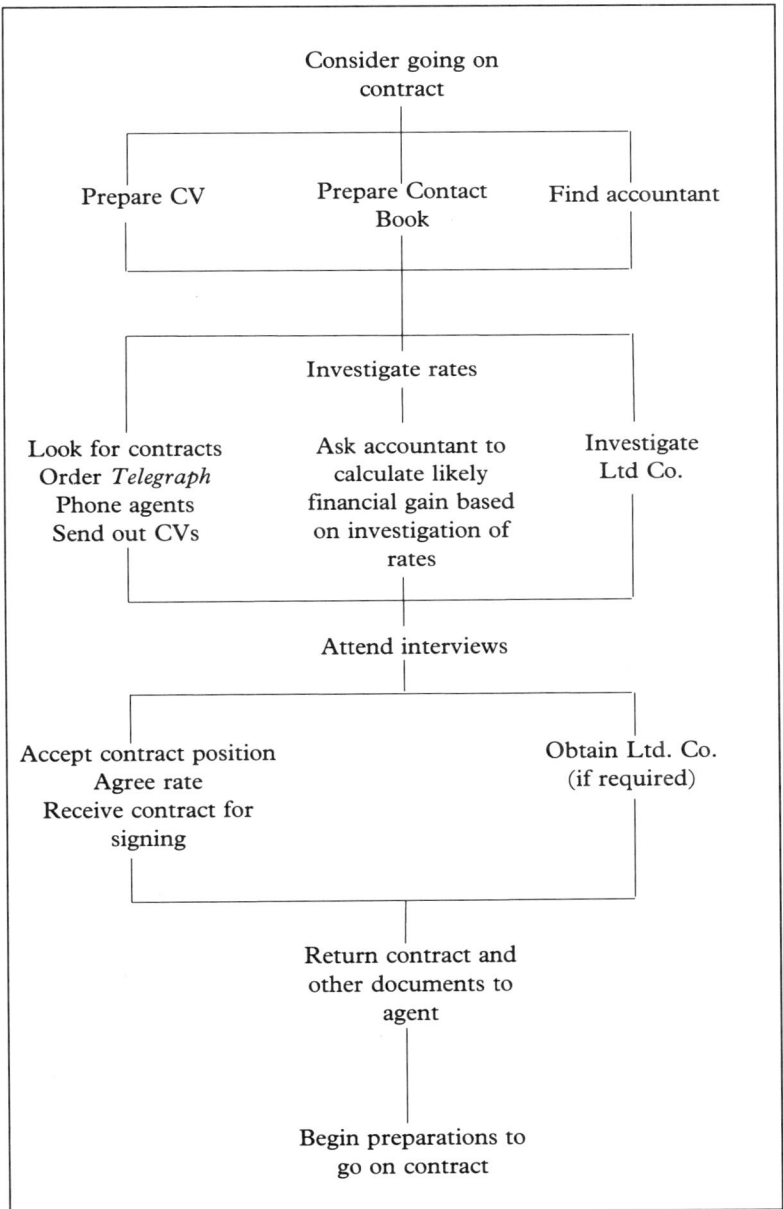

Fig. 1. Simple flowchart of the process of becoming a contractor.

Don't put yourself in the position, as many have, of being forced to delay sending a CV, attending an interview or starting a contract because you aren't ready. The job will probably go to somebody else. When a contract opportunity arises, you must be able to move quickly.

## PREPARING YOUR CV

It is a complete waste of time contacting an agent for a contract vacancy if you do not have a CV ready to send him because it is the first thing that he will ask for. The sooner he can place a contractor, the sooner he can claim his percentage. He will not wait for you.

### The importance of your CV
Your CV is:

- the most important part of your contractor's equipment

- your means of getting yourself known

- a sales brochure for yourself and the skill that you have to offer.

Your CV can make you or break you. A badly composed, garbled or illegible CV will probably go straight into the agent's waste bin. Better CVs from other applicants are dropping through his letter box every day.

If a CV is scruffy and carelessly written the chances are that the applicant is scruffy and careless too and thereby a bad risk to send to a client.

Two factors distinguish a good CV from a bad one:

- appearance
- content

### Giving your CV the correct appearance
- CVs should always be typed. Never send a handwritten CV to an agent. A well presented CV looks professional and is an encouragement for the agent to read it which, after all, is why you sent it in the first place. If you do not have a typewriter,

borrow one or find someone to do the typing for you. If the latter means paying a typing agency a modest fee, it will be money well invested.

● Better still is a CV prepared on a word processor. If you have your CV on a floppy disc it can be easily updated or altered to meet particular contingencies without having to re-do the whole thing. If you do not own or have access to a word processor, you can hire one. Look in the Yellow Pages and in your local papers.

● If another person types your CV for you, ensure that your draft copy is laid out exactly as you want it. It will waste time and possibly cost you money if the typist has to keep asking you questions or if you have to send work back for re-typing. If there are too many changes, your typing job could find itself permanently at the end of the queue.

### Arranging the content of your CV

Your CV must convey hard facts about your experience and abilities that the agent can easily compare with his clients' requirements. Note that the agent may re-arrange your CV to give it the slant he feels a particular job requires and will not want to sift through a lot of irrelevant detail. Keep it brief and to the point. Be sure to include any service in the armed forces.

Using good quality, white A4 paper, prepare your CV using the style and layout shown in the sample CV in Fig. 2.

### Notes to Fig. 2

1. Give names in natural order, e.g. Christopher J. Thompson. Do not write 'Thompson, Christopher' as this may result in your CV being filed under 'Christopher', never to be seen again.

2. If you are using a temporary address for any reason, e.g. working away, state this in your covering letter and also the date, if known, until which the temporary address will be valid.

3. Include the postcode(s).

4. Do not say 'Anytown 12234'. Give the full dialling code

CHRISTOPHER J. THOMPSON (1)
32 Evington Crescent, (2)
Mellingbury,
Bristol BS99 9XZ (3)                    01272 00000 (4)

Name of Ltd. Company (if applicable)
Company registration No.
VAT registration No.

LOGISTICS SUPPORT ANALYST—
AVIONICS/ELECTRONICS (5)
Bsc Engineering, electronics (6)

LANGUAGES SPOKEN: French, (7)

PROFESSIONAL EXPERIENCE: (8)


FLYHIGHER AVIATION LTD., BRISTOL
                                    1991–present

- Performing (9) Logistics Support Analysis (LSA) (10) of Secondary Attitude Heading Reference System, Eurobomber project (11) to MIL STD 1388 1a/2b (12) using DILSA computer program (13) to determine logistic support requirements.

- Conducting equipment Level of Repair Analysis using EDCAS program.

- Preparing project progress reports for senior management.

- Representing company at Consortium monthly meetings.

Fig. 2. Sample CV (figures in brackets refer to notes in text).

## SHOOTHARDER WEAPON COMPANY LTD., GLOUCESTER 1989–1991

- Determining maintenance support requirements to MIL STD 1388 1a/2b using SLIC computer program for Fire Control System (FCS), 100mm anti-aircraft gun for South Arabian Defence Force.

- Writing preventive and corrective maintenance task procedures in Simplified English for South Arabian maintenance crews (14).

- Travelling regularly to Al Cohol base, South Arabia (15) for customer liaison meetings and to assess maintenance training requirements.

## SEEFAR RADAR LTD., BRISTOL 1981–1989

- Designing radar transmitter/receiver systems (initial four years post-graduate experience), subsequently transferring to newly established LSA Dept, Customer Support Division (16).

- Developing logistics procedures and integrating into company working practices.

- Liaising with company engineering and computer divisions in development of dedicated logistics software (17).

## EDUCATION

Birmingham University 1979–1981
  Bsc engineering, electronics
Mellingbury Sixth Form College 1977–1979
  Passed 'A' level Physics, Applied Maths,
    Chemistry

Mellingbury Comprehensive School          1973–1977
  Passed GCSE English language, English Literature, Maths,
  French, Physics, Chemistry, Geography, Technical
  Drawing, Biology


Courses Attended

Computer Technology, day release          1983–1984
Mellingbury Adult Education Centre

Logistics Analysis course with Logistics          1985
Analysis Specialists Ltd., Exeter


DATE OF BIRTH: 21/9/66          Married. 2 children


HOBBIES AND INTERESTS:
Sailing, brass rubbing, sketching.

---

including country code from the UK if you happen to be situated abroad. The same applies to temporary telephone numbers as for temporary addresses.

Office telephone number may be added here and is essential for speed of contact but to be omitted if likely to lead to embarrassment (yours!). Most agents are highly discrete when calling applicants at work.

5. State discipline precisely. Don't just put 'Engineer'. Mr Thompson has stated that he is a 'Logistics Engineer' and has added his speciality 'Avionics/electronics'. This should save him from being bothered with enquiries for Logistics engineers, mechanics. It will save the agent's time too.

6. Give highest qualification only here. List GCSEs, etc. under Education.

7. State any special additional skills, e.g. languages spoken.

8. Give your employment record in reverse order, commencing with your current or most recent employment, with years of employment and include a short description of each job.

9. Use the present continuous to describe functions performed. This form gives a good impression of activity.

10. If your discipline is highly specialised, some agents may not be familiar with either its full title or its acronym, so use both where they first appear in your CV. For subsequent appearances use the acronym alone.

11. Name all projects. Some run for years and may provide lasting opportunities, or experience already gained may be transferable to another project being performed to similar parameters.

12. State all military and civil specifications you have used.

13. State all computer programmes in which you have competence.

14. Mention any experience in dealing with the developing world. As defence markets in the west decline and more companies seek to sell their products elsewhere, such experience could stand you in good stead.

15. Mention all work related foreign travel. It is a very good substitute for actual overseas contract experience.

16. Use your CV to demonstrate adaptability. In the sample CV Mr Thompson shows adaptability by transferring to a new technology.

17. Mr Thompson uses his CV to demonstrate his involvement in the development, rather than merely the performance of his discipline. This demonstrates initiative.

## Your growing CV

When you become a contractor you will change jobs much more frequently than in staff employment and company names will accumulate on your CV. Whilst this can indicate instability or unreliability in a staff job seeker and will certainly raise eyebrows, it is of far less importance for a contractor. A long contract will, however, look good on your CV because it shows that the client company thought well of you.

As your CV grows, perhaps to several pages, keep its size under control by gradually reducing the amount of information you give for earlier jobs.

### Never run out of CVs

When your CV is complete, keep a supply of copies handy and make sure that you can produce more when required. Always keep several with you at all times and never, ever be without any at all. It is always when you have just sent out your last hard copy that another is suddenly required and that is when your word processor or photocopier goes wrong.

### Keep your CV up-to-date at all times

Even when you are happy with your current contract and have no intention of looking for another, be ready for the moment when it comes. Updating a CV to reflect your latest experience, or rewriting part of or the whole thing to suit a change of circumstances, can take a lot longer than you might think. Don't be caught out by not having a current CV ready to send out at a moments' notice.

Finally, as you add contract situations to your CV, quote the name of the client company to whom you were contracted, not the name of the agent involved.

### Question and answer session

Q. *Should I submit my CV on a floppy disc rather than as a printout?*

A. Not without the prior agreement of the agent concerned and certainly not as a general rule.

Q. *Should I employ an agency to write my CV?*

A. Only as a very last resort. You will be charged a lot of money for a service which may not significantly improve your chances of winning a contract. Professionally prepared CV's can be spotted and some agents think that they smell of falsehood.

Q. *I am interested in contracting because I am about to be made redundant. How do I deal with this in my CV?*

A. You don't. Simply enter the details of your current employment in your CV as if no redundancy has happened/were about to happen. When it does happen, use your covering letter (see Finding Contracts) to explain that you are immediately available because your job (not you) with your last employer was made redundant. If you can de-personalise the redundancy by quoting company restructuring/takeover/loss of government orders etc., so much the better. Your instant availability could actually be advantageous.

## ESTABLISHING YOUR CONTACT BOOK

### Why have a Contact Book?

Next to your CV, your agency Contact Book is your most valuable tool. It is an expanded address book containing agents' names, addresses and telephone numbers. Properly used it can save you a lot of time and frustration when you are looking for a contract.

Many contractors manage without a Contact Book. They keep vital telephone numbers on scraps of paper which they are constantly losing. Contracts have been lost through untidy personal habits. Establish your Contact Book as soon as you decide to become a contractor. Keep it organised and you will be one move ahead of your less careful competitors.

### Creating a Contact Book

Your Contact Book should have loose leaves and tabbed dividers for easy organisation into alphabetical order. Use one page for each agent. Fig. 3 shows a suggested layout and entry headings.

You will no doubt wish to refine the layout to suit your own requirements, either by modifying a purchased address book or better still, by creating your own with a word processor. If you use A4 format you will be able to store letters in the same section as the relevant agent. A minimum of fifty pages is suggested to begin with.

> *Note:* An electronic notebook can also be used, but keep back-up copies and hard copies of all data stored.

### Keeping your Contact Book up-to-date

The first entries that you make in your Contact Book will be the details of agencies that you collect in the initial stages of becoming a contractor. Do not assume that those details are cast in bronze.

Agent's name . . . . . . . . . . . . . . . .

Agent's telephone number . . . . . . . . . . . . .

Agent's address . . . . . . . . . . . . . . . .

Agent's telefax number . . . . . . . . . . . . .

Agent's contact man . . . . . . . . . . . . . . .

Dates of contacts
e.g. telephone calls, letter to/from, etc. . . . . . . . . .

Dates CV sent . . . . . . . . . . . . . . . .

Dates CV acknowledged . . . . . . . . . . . . .

Location of contract . . . . . . . . . . . . . . .

Length of contract . . . . . . . . . . . . . . .

Type of work . . . . . . . . . . . . . . . . . .

Rate of pay . . . . . . . . . . . . . . . . . .

Notes: (including details of advertisements)

Fig. 3. Suggested layout of Contact Book.

Agencies, their contact men, addresses and telephone numbers are constantly changing. Agencies go out of business, are taken over or appear for the first time. Note any change immediately and trust nothing to memory. If you do not keep your Contact Book up-to-date, you will weaken your chances of survival.

### Case history: spending time to save time

Over the years, contractors accumulate hundreds of agency addresses, sometimes in the form of lists distributed by well meaning colleagues. Len Thomas had acquired several such lists but had been reluctant to use the addresses until he had validated them. Many appeared to be very old, much altered and pale through years of re-photocopying.

Len went to the library and checked every address against the relevant telephone directory. Already suspecting that some of his information might be out of date, he was amazed to find how many of the agencies listed had moved, changed their names, had different telephone numbers or simply disappeared without trace. He also discovered that many of the details on his lists were inaccurate in small but significant ways, perhaps in just one digit of a telephone number. From the notes that he made, Len was able to produce a far more accurate and up-to-date list. He reckoned that he had probably saved quite a lot of time, effort and expense as a result and had improved his chances of finding contracts because of accurate targeting of agents.

## EMPLOYING AN ACCOUNTANT

As soon as you begin looking for contracts you should find yourself a chartered accountant. You will need his guidance in all financial matters, especially taxation, arising from your business affairs (see Identifying Different Types of Contract).

Your accountant will maximise your profits from contracting because he knows how to 'play the system' to your benefit. He will save you far more annually than his services will cost you.

### Finding an accountant

If you intend only to work in the UK, the nearest accountant to your home will be the obvious one to give your business to. If you plan to work abroad however, you must choose an accountant experienced in the tax affairs of people who work abroad. Some specialise in nothing but this kind of work. An appropriately experienced accountant can be found by consulting:

- the Yellow Pages
- Appendix I of this book

### In the smoke or the sticks?

A small point to consider when choosing where to locate your accountant is that major urban centres usually have large and busy Inland Revenue offices whose staff will be more likely to be familiar with the affairs of people who go contracting and/or work overseas. Small, rural tax offices, not perhaps accustomed to such matters, may find your affairs a novelty and thereby take an unwarranted interest in them. This can lead to a lot of boring questions being asked, however regular the conduct of your operation.

### Question and answer session

Q. *How much is employing an accountant likely to cost me?*
A. About £1,000 per year, although some accountants specialising in providing services to contractors do claim that their costs are far less.

Q. *Are the accountant's fees tax deductible?*
A. Yes, where tax is payable.


## FINDING CONTRACTS

Contracts are not difficult to obtain once you know how to locate vacancies. These fall into two categories:

1. advertised vacancies
2. unadvertised vacancies

### Advertised vacancies

An agent will advertise a contract vacancy when he identifies an opportunity to place a contractor with a client company but can find nobody suitable or currently available from his files.

The advantage of advertised vacancies is that they are usually for fairly solid and immediate requirements; agents do not go to the expense of advertising unless they see good potential for business. The disadvantage is that hundreds of other contractors will see the advertisements too, so there will be competition.

Advertised vacancies are also a useful indication of the state of the contract market, even when you are not actually seeking a job, and are a valuable source of agency names, addresses and telephone numbers.

Note that there is also the 'advertised non-vacancy', placed by some agents when they wish to update their contractor databases, perhaps against some perceived, potential requirement, and feature phantom openings to attract CVs.

## Unadvertised vacancies

Many contractors rely on this category almost entirely, seldom needing to reply to advertisements in order to find work. They do this by making sure that their details and CVs are held on file by as many agents as possible, sometimes several hundred. As vacancies arise the agent will contact suitable people from his files and perhaps never need to advertise.

## The Contractor's Bible

The finest and time honoured way to locate vacancies and/or agents is to study the small ads in the appointments pages of the Thursday edition of the *Daily Telegraph*. This column is a market place for agents with vacancies to fill and for contractors seeking work.

*Note:* Advertisements for contractors may sometimes be found in other newspapers, in industry trade journals and in publications issued by a number of organisations (see Appendix III).

If you do not take the *Telegraph* regularly, order the Thursday edition from your newsagent or at the very least, buy a copy early in the morning. If you fail to do this you will be giving your competitors the chance to reply to ads before you. You might even find the edition sold out.

Study the small ads very carefully. Most are for contractors although staff vacancies do appear. These latter frequently quote an annual salary, not applicable to a contractor.

## Creating a snowstorm

The objective in gleaning names, addresses and telephone numbers from the paper is to place your details with as many agents as possible, i.e. to create a snowstorm of CVs. Remember that agents search their files before they advertise. If your details are not available, you cannot be contacted for the vacancy that may never be announced. When you have a list of telephone numbers, call the agents concerned.

## Talking to the agent

If you are calling purely on spec, once you have identified your discipline you will probably be told that there is no requirement at the moment but please send in your CV. Do so. You may not have got a contract but you have not wasted your time because your details will now be on file. You might receive an acknowledgement that your CV has arrived and perhaps also an agency application form to fill in. If the agent says that he does not deal in your industry or discipline, make a note to that effect in your contact book.

If you are calling about an advertised vacancy, or on spec and there happens to be a suitable, unadvertised vacancy, the agent will be only too happy to speak to you. He will certainly ask you to forward your CV to him as quickly as possible, perhaps by telefax.

*Note:* It will cost a lot of money to use a public fax service to send several CVs to dozens of agents. Only to be used in the most urgent cases.

The advantage of telephoning before you actually send in your CV is that if there is a vacancy, the agent will be able to tell his client that he has an applicant who may be suitable.

Your conversation with the agent will range over several points. If he doesn't raise them, you should. Some agents will be very forthcoming and others vague. A lot depends on how far the agent's negotiations with the client have progressed. If he sounds guarded it could be that he genuinely cannot answer your questions at this stage or that he is afraid that you might actually be a rival doing a bit of spying. Keep notes for your contact book as you discuss the following:

● *What is the job precisely?*
Requirements are often vague and subject to misinterpretation in their passage from client onwards. Find out as much as you can and make sure that the agent understands the skill that you have to offer.

● *Where is the contract located?*

The agent may be precise, if not, try to draw him out, e.g. 'on the continent' could mean anything from Amsterdam to Vienna and could make a big difference to your travelling time and expenses.

● *What is the likely duration of the contract?*

The agent will probably state an initial contract period. Ask about the likelihood of extension (see below, How Long Will It Last).

● *Who is the client?*

The agent may be cautious about revealing this too soon. Try and find out anyway.

● *Does the agent have any staff on site already?*

If the answer is 'no', the agent may be at the early stages of negotiation himself and possibly fending off dozens of competitors. Your chances are thereby reduced. If the answer is 'yes', the agent already has a relationship with the client which means that your chances are significantly enhanced.

● *What is the rate?*

(See below, Setting the Rate.)

● *Your limited company*

(See Running a Limited Company in Chapter 3.) The agent will amost certainly ask whether you have a limited company. If you don't have one already, simply say that you will have one organised by the time you reach the stage of signing a contract . . . and be certain that you have. Do not ask the agent a lot of questions about limited companies; you might frighten him off.

● *Third Party Insurance*

The agent may remind you that legislation requires your company to have Employer's Liability and Public Liability Insurance. Your local insurance broker will arrange this for you. It will cost you from £100 per annum for £1,000,000 of cover for any one event. Tell the agent that you have this in hand.

● *Your availability*

It could cost you a contract if the requirement is immediate and you have to work out a month's notice in your present job. You might be able to reduce the notice period by including unused holiday entitlement or volunteering for redundancy, but never resign until you have a signed contract in your hand. If the agent cannot wait, send him your CV anyway and look around for another contract with a more leisurely start date.

- *Security clearance*

Security clearance is required for many defence related contracts. If you have had clearance recently, there will usually be no problem in obtaining further clearance. If you have never had clearance or have recently returned from abroad, delays of several months in obtaining clearance can occur. Such delays can lose you contracts.

## Sounding positive

Whatever questions the agent asks you to determine your suitability for a vacancy, he will learn a lot about you from the tone of your reply. A positive attitude helps even if you are negotiating for your first contract, perhaps abroad, and don't feel confident because you are dealing with an unknown quantity. If you ask questions about which train you should catch to get to work, or what 'abroad' is actually like, the agent will wonder if he ought to find some other, more experienced person.

## Always get a name

Before you conclude your conversation, make sure that you have noted the name of the person you have been talking to, or if calling on spec and perhaps speaking only to a telephonist, the name of the person to whom you should send your CV.

## Sending in your CV

When you submit your CV, enclose a covering letter which should include the following:

- If you are following up a phone call, remind the agent of your conversation with him.

- If pursuing an advertised vacancy, state where and when seen and mention any reference number included in the advertisement.

- Emphasise any points or experience that you consider particularly qualifies you for the vacancy in question.

- Staple your letter to the front of your CV to prevent separation and place both, unfolded (it looks tidier and is easier to read) in an A4 envelope.

- Be sure to include in the address the name of the person you want your CV to reach.

## Waiting for results

If you have submitted your CV in respect of a definite requirement, the agent will probably tell you when you should expect to hear from him again. He does not, after all, want you looking for another job if he thinks he can place you with a client. Remember though, that he may have sent other CVs besides yours for the client to make his own short list selection.

If you hear nothing when you expect to, call the agent again. He may tell you that he is still waiting to hear from the client but that something should happen soon. Don't attach too much importance to the 'soon'. Things can move very slowly until the client himself acts and then the agent will want to arrange an interview as quickly as possible.

If however, a series of encouraging contacts is followed by a Deafening Silence, it usually means that the trail has gone cold and, as sometimes happens, the agent has omitted to tell you. Don't worry; you've just been unlucky this time. It could also mean that the agent has been unsuccessful rather than you.

Similarly, don't be surprised if an agent to whom you have previously submitted a CV advertises for somebody of your discipline without contacting you. This need not mean that you have been eliminated but rather overlooked.

## Case history: a contract almost lost

Eric Hughes telephoned an agent who was advertising for a technical author in nuclear handling. The agent was enthusiastic about Eric's experience and asked him to submit his CV. Encouraged to expect a quick response, Eric became puzzled after a week of silence.

Eric phoned again, reminded the agent of his existence and their previous conversation and expressed his surprise that he had heard nothing more. The agent said that Eric's CV must have got lost in the post but as he had several others he had submitted them to the client instead, assuming that Eric had found another job or had lost interest. On Eric's insistence, the agent asked him to hold while he 'looked in the other office'. Minutes later he returned, apologising that his secretary was on holiday and that the temp has misfiled Eric's details. Now that he had found it, he would fax the CV to the client immediately and was still hopeful on Eric's behalf as his was the most suitable CV that he had received. Eric subsequently got the job, but has often pondered that he might not have done had he not taken the trouble to chase the agent.

## Persevering

You may be lucky enough to see a perfect ad in the first paper that you open and a short while later find yourself on contract in some exotic part of the world at a vary high rate of pay. It doesn't often happen that way but it can. More likely you will spend several months contacting agents before you land a contract. Keep trying. Study the papers constantly. Record each advertisement, each agent's details and the essentials of every telephone conversation in your Contact Book.

Above all, never give up. Sooner or later you will find yourself invited to attend an interview.

## Finally, a caveat

There are a few Don'ts to observe when hunting for contracts:

- Don't pay too much attention to the agent who asks you to guarantee that if he promotes your application you will not seek employment elsewhere. You might miss other opportunities while you are being strung along. Ask him if he can guarantee to get you a contract.

- Don't, under any circumstances, pay an agent to find you a contract. If he were any good at all he would make his money from the client. If he can't find you a job in the normal way, paying him won't make him a better agent.

- Don't listen to the agent who wants you to hand in your notice immediately, or leave without notice at all, on his certainty of a contract. You may think that you are throwing away the chance of a contract, perhaps after months of searching. Take a deep breath and try elsewhere.

- Don't believe the agent who says that there are actually several vacancies so get your friends to send in their CVs too, even if you are offered a cash incentive. There may be only one vacancy and it could go to a friend who is more immediately available than you.

● Don't tell anyone that you are even looking for a contract, let alone when you have the scent of one. You might find them beating a path to the agent's door. It's amazing how empty friendship can be when money is involved.

### Question and answer session

Q. *I have been approached by two different agents regarding the same vacancy. What do I do?*

A. This happens all the time. Unless you have a preference, let both agents submit your CV and allow the client to choose which agency he would rather deal with.

Q. *I am a components engineer and I never seem to see advertisements for my discipline. Am I wasting my time looking for contracts?*

A. Not necessarily. Your discipline is fairly rare and agents may not wish to spend on advertising for people they think they cannot find, even if there are vacancies available. It's up to you to advertise your existence.

Q. *I am a draughtsman. I have called dozens of agents and sent out loads of CVs. Although some agents have been encouraging, I never seem to hear anything more. Am I doing something wrong or should I just give up?*

A. Definitely don't give up. If there is a problem it could be simply that you are competing in a well populated discipline. More precise targeting may be required. Next time you phone around the agencies, ask what the market place is seeking and see how you can adapt your CV to meet current requirements.

## ATTENDING INTERVIEWS

One of the quirks of contracting is that the client who is going to pay you a great deal of money for your services may never ask you to attend an interview at all. There are two reasons for this:

32 Evington Crescent
Mellingbury
Bristol BC99 9XZ
22 July 199X

Mr B. Goldmine
Rent-a-Whizz Ltd
Industry House
Cavern St
Liverpool L105 5YZ

Dear Mr Goldmine

**LOGISTICS ENGINEERS**

Further to our telephone conversation on 21 July 199X, I have pleasure in forwarding my current CV to you and would be pleased to hear of any suitable contract vacancies.

I am available, subject to one month's notice, for contracts in the UK or overseas and I have current Ministry of Defence security clearance.

I would be pleased to attend client interviews at short notice.

My office telephone number is 01272 XXXXX and my home number 01272 00000.

Yours sincerely

Christopher J. Thompson

Fig. 4. Writing on spec.

32 Evington Crescent
Mellingbury
Bristol BC99 9XZ
22 July 199X

Mr B. Goldmine
Rent-a-Whizz Ltd
Industry House
Cavern St
Liverpool L105 5YZ

Dear Mr Goldmine

**LOGISTICS ENGINEERS—GERMANY**

Further to our telephone conversation on 21 July 199X regarding your advertisement in the *Daily Telegraph* of the same date, I have pleasure in forwarding my CV to you as requested.

As your client is engaged upon the same project as my current employer, i.e. Eurobomber, I believe that my experience plus familiarity with the standards and specifications used will enable me to make a useful contribution to his programme.

My availability is one month and I have current Ministry of Defence security clearance.

My office telephone number is 01272 XXXXX and my home number 01272 00000.

Yours sincerely

Christopher J. Thompson

Fig. 5. Writing for an advertised vacancy.

1. Sometimes it is impractical for the client and contractor to meet because of distance.
2. The agent often carries out interviews on behalf of his client.

Depending on circumstance, therefore, there is a sliding scale of degree of interview which can be summarised thus:

- Agent interviews applicants by telephone and makes final selection himself.

- Agent and client interview applicants by telephone.

- Agent interviews applicants by telephone and client interviews applicants personally at his (client's) premises.

- Both agent and client conduct personal interviews at their respective premises.

- Agent interviews by telephone and arranges for client to conduct further interviews at a mutually convenient location. This method is commonly used for overseas contracts and usually entails the client travelling to the UK to carry out interviews.

### Arranging an interview
If a client interview is to take place, either at his premises or some other location, the agent will either telephone details of the appointment to you or confirm them in writing (see Fig. 6).

### Some interview pointers
While it is not the purpose of this section to dwell on interview technique, a subject upon which many books have been written (see Further Reading), there are a number of points specific to contract interviews that you should bear in mind.

### Beware the unexpected second interview
If the agent conducts interviews on his client's behalf, ensure that his endorsement is final. Don't leave your former job to arrive on site thinking the contract in your pocket to be your guarantee of employment, and then find yourself rejected and on the next plane home (at your expense). This has actually happened.

Rent-a-Whizz Ltd
Industry House
Cavern St
Liverpool L105 5YZ
5 August 199X

Mr C. J. Thompson
32 Evington Crescent
Mellingbury
Bristol BC99 9XZ

Dear Chris

Further to our recent telephone conversation I have pleasure in confirming interview details for a forthcoming contract in Germany.

Herr D. Weiss will be pleased to meet you in the Stagecoach Hotel, Bath Road, Bristol at 7.30 p.m. on Friday 12 August 199X. Please ask for him at the hotel reception. I enclose a map of the area with the hotel marked.

Please call this office if you need any more information.

Wishing you the best of luck and please call me on Monday morning with your impressions.

Yours sincerely,

B. Goldmine

Fig. 6. Agent's letter confirming interview arrangements.

## And another surprise

A less drastic but still unsettling experience is to be told by the client that the job is yours, although you will not be working for the agent who sent you to the interview but through another named by the client. The reason for this is fairly obvious; the client, or at least the interviewer, has an 'arrangement' with his favoured agent. How you react to this depends on whether you are feeling ethical or pragmatic at the time.

## Being ready

Many people like to take a break between jobs but when you are close to winning a contract, avoid saying that you would like to take some time off before you start. Remember that the agent will be:

- thinking of his cash flow
- worrying about rivals.

He will want you on site a.s.a.p. If you prevaricate, he may forget you and try somebody else.

## Case history: war waits for no man

Called by his agent after attending an interview, Keith Jackson was told that the job was his and that a contract would be in the post as soon as some details had been sorted out with the client. The agent expected the contract to start two or three weeks hence so Keith decided to do some long overdue decorating while he was waiting.

Three and a half weeks later, Keith received a call from the agent who said that the contract was due to start on the following Monday and the contract documentation would be posted immediately. Keith replied that he really needed another week to finish his decorating.

In the event, the contract documentation never did arrive and when Keith repeatedly telephoned the agent he ran straight into the Deafening Silence. He later learned that the contract had gone to another, more worldy-wise contractor.

## Guarding costs

Whereas interview expenses for UK based contracts are seldom offered, expenses for interviews conducted abroad should be paid. Note the following:

- Beware attending an interview abroad unless you have a return air ticket paid for by somebody else.

- Check that accommodation has been arranged if you are to stay abroad overnight.

- Don't listen to an agent who says that you should claim expenses from the client when you arrive, or from himself when you return. If you don't get the job, the matter of your expenses could drag on, unresolved, for ever.

### Checking contract duration

An interview with a client is a good opportunity to assess the likely length of the contract. Your own professional experience could tell you that there might be more work than can be done within the proposed contract initial period, thus presenting potential for contract extension.

### Eyeing conditions

An interview at the client's premises will also enable you to check working conditions, which on the Continent tend to be rather better than in the UK. If you have any doubts about what you are letting yourself in for, you may wish to insist on an on-site interview, distance permitting, if one is not offered.

### Case history: look before you leap

In recent times a number of contractors started work at a factory in Edinburgh after telephone interviews only. The working conditions proved to be so cramped, dilapidated and draughty and the office atmosphere so bad that within a very few months most of the contractors had left, despite the prospect of several years work. Many said that if they had attended interviews they would have seen how squalid the place was and would never have been prepared to work there.

The project continues but the contractor drop-out rate is so high that the site concerned is gaining a reputation as one to be avoided. The agencies are kept busy trying to fill constantly recurring vacancies.

### After the interview

Once you have passed an interview and are satisfied with the work, the rate (see below, Setting the Rate) and the likely duration (see below, How Long will it Last?) of the assignment, the agent will not waste any time in getting your signature on a contract document.

## Question and answer session

Q. *What should I take to an interview?*
A. The following:

- copy of your CV (it isn't unknown for an interviewer to be unable to lay hands on his copy of your CV and may wish to refer to it— he will be more impressed with your efficiency than his own!)

- copies of references and qualifications (just in case as these are very rarely asked for)

- copy of your birth certificate (usually for security purposes)

- samples of your work (security and confidentiality considerations permitting)

- notepad

- agent's letter confirming interview arrangements and map.

Q. *Will I be told at an interview whether or not I have the job?*
A. Sometimes, yes. You are actually more likely to be told that you have the job than that you have not. Clients normally leave the agent to pass on the bad news.

Q. *What should I do immediately after an interview with a client?*
A. Phone the agent a.s.a.p. He will be anxious to know how you fared.

Q. *Following a very positive interview with a client who says that he wants me but warns that raising the internal paperwork may take some weeks, I have been offered another interview elsewhere with another agent. Should I go?*
A. Definitely. The client at your last interview sounds sincere but matters may not rest entirely in his hands and there's many a slip, etc.

Q. *Should I discuss rates with the client at interview?*
A. No. Many agents will advise against this in their letter confirming interview arrangements. The setting of your rate is between yourself and the agent, who will negotiate his own charge with the client.

## SETTING THE RATE

### Will it be worth it?

The aspiring contractor has a particular problem in knowing what rate of pay to expect or to ask. In particular he will need to know whether contracting will be worthwhile in terms of enhanced income and adequate compensation for the inconvenience of living and working away from home.

One approach is to ask your accountant to calculate for you the minimum hourly rate that will enable you to meet your personal aspirations, taking your individual financial circumstances into consideration. He will need to know the expenses (travel/lodgings/subsistence etc) that you will incur whilst on contract. Experience indicates that these will be roughly;

UK contract expenses:                    £10,000 p.a.

European contract expenses:              £15,000 p.a.

*Notes:* Calculations should be based on the following most likely scenarios:

(i)    limited company basis
(ii)   single status away from home
(iii)  tax free status abroad

Once you have established your minimum hourly rate, you will know immediately whether the rate for a given contract will be viable for you. Do not reveal your minimum acceptable rate when you start negotiating; it is purely for your guidance and may well be lower than the rate for the contract under discussion.

There are further steps that you can take to give you an idea of what your rate should be.

● During your conversations with agents whom you call on spec, ask the rate for your discipline. You may not always get a direct answer (the agent might think that you are a snooping competitor) but if you ask the question often enough, you will soon gain a broad idea of your market value.

- If you are discussing an actual vacancy with an agent, simply ask the question about rates. He may be able to give you a precise or at least a general figure, but if he is still negotiating with his client, he may be unable or unwilling to quote a rate. He may even ask the rate you want to see how much he can charge the client after he has added his percentage.

If you have a contract already or have just left one, you may be asked for details of your most recent rate. Keep this information to yourself. The amount that you are or were earning has no more relevance than the price of your last car has on the price of a new one. The market place and your position in it are what counts.

Once you have reached the stage where you are about to sign a contract and therefore know the rate of pay (assuming it to be greater than your known absolute minimum), go back to your accountant and ask him for a fresh calculation based on that rate. This will enable you to assess the likely benefit that contracting will bring you.

## Is it possible to haggle?

Certainly, and the longer you remain a contractor, the better you will become at negotiating your rate because:

- you will know your own value

- you will be familiar with the market

- your increasing wealth will enable you to turn down contracts that do not pay the rate that you want.

Be careful though, of overplaying your hand until you have gained some contract experience. Contracting, like any other business, has to be learned. Additionally, some contracts offer no room for negotiation because the client has set both the rate and the agent's percentage mark-up. In this case the agent will probably advise you of the situation. If the rate in question falls beneath your known minimum, it should not be too difficult to turn it down, although even a poor rate can be an attractive alternative to unemployment. It will at least give you a breathing space while you search for something better.

### Question and answer session

Q.  *I have been approached by two different agents for the same job but at different rates. Why?*

A.  Both agents may have the same charge rate to the client but apply different hourly rates to the contractor, i.e. one is making a bigger profit out of you than the other. Alternatively, one agent could be trying to undercut a rival and still retain his percentage profit by offering you a lower rate.

Q.  *Can I improve my rate after a contract has begun?*

A.  Yes, in time. An agent will seek to increase his charge to the client annually and you should benefit accordingly. Resigning can also bring an improvement in rate although this course is not recommended unless you really mean it.

Q.  *Can I change agents during a contract to improve my rate?*

A.  This is sometimes done but rarely without acrimony.

## HOW LONG WILL IT LAST?

This is the question that all contractors ask when they are discussing a new assignment with an agent. It isn't worth leaving a staff position for a contract that may only last a short while, and if you are going abroad you will not be able to take advantage of tax benefits if you are away for less than a year (see Applying The One Sixth Rule in Chapter 3).

The agent's reply to the question may be:

● initial contract of so many weeks or months, extendable by equal periods

● so many weeks or months, not extendable

● initial period with provision for extension as required, length of extension unspecified.

The duration of a contract often depends upon the completion of the project for which the contractor is hired. Many projects overrun their target completion date and unless any contractor involved has been shown to be incompetent, he is usually kept on. In fact, the longer he stays, the more likely he is to remain as his accumulating experience increases his value to the client.

## Staying the course

Signing a contract for a given period is not a guarantee that you will have employment for the whole of that period. You and the client may not suit each other or there may be problems that cause the project to shut down. This is one of the risks of contracting. Contractors are hired for their expertise and because they are easier to dispense with than permanent staff.

If your contract does collapse you will find it almost impossible to make a claim against your agent or the client company. The best course is to swallow your annoyance and try again somewhere else. Collapsing contracts are however, very rare.

If your contract is extended, you will not usually have to sign any more paperwork. Your original contract will probably contain a clause making this unnecessary.

Note that **the majority of contracts last far longer than expected.**

## OBTAINING RESIDENCE AND WORK PERMITS

Residence and work permits are official sanctions granted by the authorities of a host country for a foreign national to live and work in that country.

Work permits are not required for British citizens to work in the member states of the EU.

Residence permits are necessary in all EU member states except Eire and may be obtained after arrival, but vary in application as follows:

| | |
|---|---|
| After 3 months | —France, Germany, Spain, Denmark |
| After 6 months | —Belgium |
| Within 3 days | —Italy |
| Within 8 days | —the Netherlands |

Registration of residence may be made at the town hall, immigration office, local council office or police station according to the country concerned. Ask when you arrive.

In any other country that you are likely to be sent to, you will almost certainly require work and residence permits and possibly a visa as well. If you are negotiating with an agent for a contract in a country outside the EU, the matter of permits will be raised. If not, you must raise it.

### Never go without necessary permits

It is very unwise to leave the UK until you are completely satisfied that you will not find yourself an illegal immigrant when you arrive. It is a very uncomfortable feeling being in a foreign country when you know you shouldn't be there. In the worst case it will be you who is arrested, not your agent.

Most agents but not all, will be meticulous about permits because a contractor who runs into trouble with the local authorities will not be earning the agent his percentage when he, the contractor is deported.

### If in doubt

It is a great temptation to believe what you are told, particularly when you have the scent of a lucrative contract and the agent is telling you what you would like to hear. Be very wary if you are told that:

- You will have to obtain your own work permit when you arrive.

  *Note:* Some contract clauses will state that you must organise your own work permit. This is fine because you know where you stand, and quite different from an unwritten 'sort it out yourself' situation.

- The client will arrange all that after you arrive.

- You can work in the host country for a certain period before you have to regularise your position.

If you have cause for suspicion, contact the embassy/consulate/high commission of the country concerned and ask for the regulations to be spelled out. Better still, write and ask for a written reply. If the answer you receive does not accord with what the agent is telling you, inform him of your findings. If he threatens to find somebody else for the job, let him. He might be doing you a favour.

In the majority of cases where work permits are required, they should be obtained before you arrive in the host country.


## Case history: a contractor and an impatient agent

Before signing a contract for an assignment in Johannesburg, Mark Rolands telephoned the South African embassy and learned that he would require a work permit before his arrival. The agent assured Mark that the client was arranging permits and that because of the urgency of the situation would meet Mark on arrival, with his permit, at the immigration office.

Against his better judgement Mark signed the contract, collected his ticket and made the long flight south. Upon landing at Jan Smuts airport his suppressed fears were realised when he was refused admission as he had neither work permit nor return ticket. There was no sign of the client's representative nor could Mark reach the company by phone as it was past office hours. He tried further useless remonstration and explanation with the immigration officials but was told that his only course of action was to pay a heavy deposit against his eventual departure. Unsure now whether there was even a job for him, Mark decided not to risk any of his own money in somebody else's muddle, whatever its cause. He thus chose to be deported and was put on the flight back to London.

Mark did eventually return to South Africa, but this time he refused to be hurried or to leave the UK until he had every required document in his hand.


## Question and answer session

Q.  *I have begun negotiating for a one year contract abroad but have learned from the embassy concerned that I can only have a work permit for three months, non-renewable. It is a condition of the contract that I should arrange my own permit. What should I do?*

A.  Don't despair immediately; this situation is not uncommon. Advise the agent of your findings and ask him to consult the client who, after all needs you, may have faced this problem before and may know of different paths through his country's bureaucracy.

Q. *What do I need to take with me for registration in an EU country?*
A. You will certainly need your passport, possibly copies of your birth and marriage certificates, conceivably a copy of your contract and/or a letter from the client confirming that you are working for him and therefore able to support yourself, and a plentiful supply of passport photographs.

Q. *Do I need to de-register on the way out?*
A. Yes, and this requirement should not be ignored however great the temptation at the end of a contract just to jump in your car and disappear. If you subsequently try to re-register in that country and your earlier omission comes to light, you could be fined.

## SIGNING A CONTRACT DOCUMENT

### Reading the small print
After a successful interview, you will receive a contract document for signing. Do not allow elation to cloud your judgement. While most contracts are perfectly innocuous, they do differ widely in their length, complexity and degree of obligation placed upon you. Read the document very carefully and if you are concerned about any of its conditions, call the agent for clarification.

### What will I find in a typical contract document?
Space does not permit the inclusion of a complete specimen as contracts often run to many pages and, as previously stated, vary considerably.

Contract documentation will include a covering letter (see Fig. 7) and two copies of the contract itself. The letter will confirm your appointment to a client company and request that you return one signed copy to the agent plus copies of your company's:

- Certificate of Incorporation
- VAT Certificate
- Certificate of Employer's and Third Party Liability insurance
- bank details.

The contract document itself will typically include the following clauses:

● *'Services'*

Defining the service/discipline/function that the contractor will perform for the client.

● *'Reimbursement'*

Confirming the rate of pay agreed between the contractor and the agent.

● *'Definitions'*

Defining affected parties, i.e.:

—the client company

—the agent (often called the company or consultant)

—the sub-contractor (your limited company) and its contract staff (you, the contractor, used hereon for simplicity).

● *'Validity'*

Stating that:

—if any part of the contract becomes invalid, the rest will remain in force

—all variations shall be confirmed in writing by the contracting parties

—the contract conditions supersede all previous oral and written agreements.

● *'Operating Basis'*

Stating that:

—the client company will define the service required and alone shall allocate work and supervise contract staff

—the contractor warrants that his CV is accurate in its contents

—the contractor will perform his duties professionally and diligently

—the contractor will observe the client company's rules, procedures and safety regulations.

● *'Location'*

Defining the contractor's place(s) of work.

● *'Duration'*

Stating:

—commencement date

—length or initial period of contract.

Rent-a-Whizz Ltd
Industry House
Cavert St
Liverpool L105 5YZ
16 August 199X

Mr C. J. Thompson
32 Evington Crescent
Mellingbury
Bristol BC99 9XZ

Dear Chris

Following your interview with Herr D. Weiss, we are pleased to confirm your appointment as Logistics Engineer to Unfall Aviation GmbH, Munich, Germany. The assignment will commence on Monday 17 September 199X. Air tickets and final travel instructions will be forwarded to you shortly.

Enclosed are two copies of the contract. Please sign and date both copies and return one to this office together with copies of your company's Certificate of Incorporation, Certificate of VAT registration and Certificate of Employer's and Third Party Liability insurance. We also require details of your company's bank account, i.e. name and address of bank; bank code; account number. If you have any specific instructions regarding payment, perhaps you would be kind enough to inform us.

We also enclose some timesheets. Please complete one time sheet per month and obtain Herr Weiss's signature in the space provided. Send the timesheet plus your company's invoice to this office.

Should you have any queries, please do not hesitate to contact me.

Yours sincerely,


B. Goldmine

Fig. 7. Letter confirming a contract appointment.

● *'Travel'*

Stating that:

—the contractor will bear the cost of his own travel to and from work, except if he is working abroad when the agent will supply him with an air ticket (or an equivalent sum) at the commencement and termination of the contract

—that the contractor will be reimbursed by the client for receipted travel expenses, including use of the contractor's own car, incurred on the client's behalf.

● *'Confidentiality'*

Stating that the contractor will:

—safeguard the client's confidentiality, secrecy, trademarks, patents, etc.

—will surrender all documentation and materials to the client at the end of the assignment

—will not reveal his rate of pay to anyone.

● *'Timesheets/Invoices/Payment'*

Stating that:

—timesheets countersigned by the client must be sent to the agent weekly/monthly plus the contractor's invoice for that period

—payment will be for hours worked only

—overtime will be paid at the same rate as normal time

—the contractor will observe the client's working hours except otherwise by agreement.

● *'Income Tax/National Insurance'*

Stating that:

—the (ltd. co.) contractor is responsible for paying his tax and NI contributions and not the agent.

● *'Health and Safety at Work'*

Stating that:

—the contractor will strictly observe the Health & Safety at Work Act 1974 (UK contracts, possibly local regulations overseas).

● *'Liability'*

Stating that:

—the contractor must provide his own Employer's and Public Liability insurance.

● *'Termination'*

Stating that:

—if the assignment is extended beyond any stated initial period, the same terms and conditions will apply

—if the contract between the agent and the client is terminated, the contractor's assignment will cease immediately

—either party may terminate the contract by giving notice (usually one month)

—the contractor may be dismissed if his services are unsatisfactory or if he misbehaves

—the agent may withhold final payments to the contractor until the client has paid the agent and the agent may deduct from final payment, any liabilities incurred by the contractor

> *Note:* Be careful regarding any clause resembling the above. If you (or your solicitor) have reservations, don't sign until it is amended.

—the termination of the contract shall not prejudice any accrued rights or liabilities of either party.

● *'Policy'*

Stating that:

—the contractor will not work for anybody else during the contract period

—the contractor will not work for the client for a given period (usually six months) after the termination of the contract, except through the agent or with his written permission.

● *'Applicable Law'*

Stating that:

—the contract is subject to the Laws of England and the jurisdiction of the High Court of England and Wales.

● *'Force Majeure'*

Stating that:

—in the case of war, insurrection, flood, fire, strike, etc., either party may terminate the contract

—the contractor will be paid only up to that termination.

## Objectionable clauses

While it is not possible to list every condition that might cause objection, there are some possibilities that require caution, for example:

- Any clause stating that you will be responsible for mistakes found in your work for any period after the termination of your employment. This is tantamount to accepting responsibility for mistakes that you may not have made or may have innocently perpetuated as a result of another's errors. If the onus of responsibility were to pass down to you for say, the crash of an aircraft, you would require professional indemnity insurance whose premiums would be prohibitively expensive. If you have any concerns regarding this point, consult your solicitor.

- Any clause referring to a terminal bonus for contracts within the UK or Europe. Terminal bonuses are commonly applied to locations outside Europe where distance makes it impractical for the contractor to come home frequently. Under such conditions some contractors get fed up or homesick and resign or even break their contracts. In Europe, where trips home can be made at almost any time, there is no need for contractual pressure to keep contractors on site. A terminal bonus is not a prize in any case, but simply a form of deferred payment.

- Any clause quoting a daily, rather than an hourly rate. One justification for the daily rate is that it requires less administration for the client in the checking of contractors' timesheets. The catch for the contractor is that the daily rate, based on a nominal number of hours per day, takes 'an average amount of overtime into account'. While in some cases the daily rate can be and is fairly applied, recent reports confirm that it is also being widely abused. Some contractors are being pressured (under threat of dismissal) to work totally unreasonable amounts of overtime, effectively unpaid.

## Making amendments

Most agents will accept reasonable amendment to their contracts documents. Some may express impatience with your caution because they will be anxious for you to start work as soon as possible. If the agent is uncooperative or bullying in his attitude, consult a solicitor. If he confirms your misgivings and the agent, knowing that you have taken legal advice, still refuses to accept amendments, don't sign. You will probably have lost a job but may have saved yourself trouble in the long run. There is always another contract.

## When you have signed

Once you are satisfied that you can accept the conditions of the contract, sign the two copies and return one to the agent. Keep your copy with you when you go. (See Chapter 3 for your business obligations according to the type of contract you have signed, i.e. limited company, PAYE, etc.)

Unless they were sent with the contract documentation, you may have to wait a few days for final travel instructions/air tickets if appropriate, etc. You are now a contractor; it only remains to go (see Chapter 4, Going on Contract).

## Question and answer session

Q. *My agent has told me that I have won a contract and that he and the client wish me to start work immediately, although the necessary paperwork, including the contract documentation, has not yet been raised because of 'administrative delays'. What should I do?*

A. This can occasionally happen but be guided by your instincts. If you do decide to start work, at least obtain a letter from the agent requesting you to do so and confirming that the requisite paperwork will follow shortly.

Q. *On reading the conditions of a contract that I have received for a project in Germany, I find a clause stating that I will be paid when the agent and client have received payment for their product or services. The agent says first payments are normally made about two months after contract commencement. Should I sign?*

A. Definitely not. Although the agent is to be commended for making you aware of the situation (which is better than expecting to be paid sooner and then being disappointed), he is reflecting a contractual condition imposed on him by the client who either may be expecting problems with his own cash flow or is just plain difficult to work for. Leave well alone.

Q. *Am I bound to remain with a contract for its entire duration, however long that may prove to be?*

A. No. All contracts should contain resignation clauses but the client will obviously be concerned, and may well seek assurance at interview, that contractors hired for specific, initial tasks shall see those tasks to completion. It is not good for the contractor's credibility if, except for the most compelling of reasons, he leaves a task uncompleted.

## CHECKLIST

1. Is your CV prepared and ready to go?
2. Do you have plenty of copies of your CV?
3. Have you established your contact book?
4. Have you located an accountant?
5. Have you ensured your copy of the Thursday *Daily Telegraph*?
6. Do you have a list of questions ready to ask agents when you contact them?
7. Are you ready to form a limited company if necessary?
8. Have you investigated Employer's and Public Liability insurance?
9. Have you calculated the likely financial advantage to yourself of becoming a contractor?
10. Have you thoroughly read and understood the conditions of your contract, and if so, do you feel that you can sign with confidence?

# 3
# Managing the Business End

This chapter considers the following:

- different types of contract
- buying and running a limited company
- taxation
- social security and national insurance contributions (NIC)
- the 'one sixth rule' governing tax free status abroad
- keeping accounts
- making the best of the money

There is more to being a successful contractor than simply earning a lot of money. Contracting is a business with administrative responsibilities and legal obligations concerning taxation and social security which the permanent staff employee does not have to bother with because his employer does most of it for him. As a contractor you will have to carry some of the administrative burden yourself, but this will be much eased by your accountant.

## DIFFERENT TYPES OF CONTRACT

Contracts vary in the way they are set up according to location, likely duration and the preferences of agent, client and contractor. The nature and quantity of administration that the contractor has to perform is a direct reflection of the type of contract imposed on or chosen by him, e.g. he may be offered the choice of limited company or PAYE status, or may prefer to operate through either a UK or offshore limited company.

Fig. 8 lists the main contract types and refers to other sections in the book that detail the administration that the contract type entails. While further types of contract exist, and other variations are constantly emerging to comply with particular local conditions

**1. UK contract**
Contractor hired by UK agent on PAYE basis.
See—Tax and Social Security

**2. UK contract**
Contractor's own limited company hired by UK agent.
See—Owning and Running a Limited Company
    —Tax and Social Security
    —Keeping Accounts

**3. Overseas contract**
Contractor hired by agent on PAYE basis.
See—Tax and Social Security
    —Applying the One Sixth Rule
    —Keeping Accounts

**4. Overseas contract**
Contractor's own UK based limited company hired by
    UK agent.
See—Owning and Running a Limited Company
    —Tax and Social Security
    —Applying the One Sixth Rule
    —Keeping Accounts

**5. Overseas contract**
Contractor's own offshore limited company hired by UK
    agent.
See—Owning and Running a Limited Company
    —Tax and Social Security
    —Applying the One Sixth Rule
    —Keeping Accounts

**6. Overseas contract**
Contractor hired by agent on PAYE basis.
See—Tax and Social Security
    —Applying the One Sixth Rule
    —Keeping Accounts

**7. Overseas contract**
Contractor hired by UK or foreign agent.
See—Tax and Social Security

Fig. 8. Types of contract.

and changing legislation, the table shows those that you are most likely to encounter.

## Self employment

Although self employment (as opposed to PAYE or limited company) is possible under certain circumstances, it is excluded from the list above because the 1974 Finance Act restrains an employer from paying regular sums of money to a self employed person. This is a result of the tax abuses of the 'lump' system that used to be common within the building industry. Ironically, building workers can obtain exemptions from the restraints that are not available to others. Particular restrictions apply to agencies in the hiring of self employed persons.

## Going direct

An alternative to working through an agent is to go direct, i.e. to market your services yourself to client companies. Although a few contractors do go direct (and thereby enjoy the financial bonus of claiming the agent's percentage of the charge rate for themselves), there are disadvantages:

- You will not have the agent's contacts with diverse client companies.

- You will need to negotiate the terms of your own contract with the client and this requires specific expertise and guidance.

- Some client companies refuse to deal directly with contractors.

- Large companies do not move quickly and you could spend a lot of time waiting for a promising contact to materialise when you could have been working elsewhere through an agent.

- You might find your client very slow in making payments to you.

Try going direct by all means but be prepared to find it considerably more difficult and time consuming than finding work through an agent. You may indeed come to appreciate the true value of the agent's role in contracting.

## OWNING AND RUNNING A LIMITED COMPANY

The list of contract types shows that the majority are operated on a limited company basis. When you go into contracting you will need to own a limited company, more likely sooner than later.

There is nothing alarming about owning and running a limited company as long as you understand what is involved. All the hard work will be done by your accountant anyway. Owning a limited company is only a worry if you are suddenly forced into it in order to get a contract and without understanding what is involved.

When the contract arises that requires you to obtain a company, be ready to do so but don't actually part with the formation or purchase fee until you are certain of getting the contract.

### Why have a limited company?

Quite simply, because most agents will insist on it. There are several reasons for this:

1. To save the agent money. It is cheaper for an agent to employ a contractor on a limited company basis, albeit at a higher rate than PAYE, than to pay the employer's Class 1 NIC. PAYE employment also involves a lot of administrative work for the agent who may after all, only hire a contractor for a limited period. Every time an agent places a contractor with a client, all the official paper work relating to that contractor's employment, notably for taxation and insurance, has to be raised and dealt with. Coping with the paper work means that the agent has to employ extra staff whose wages increase his overheads and eat into his profitability.

2. To distance the agent from tax and NIC problems. Not all contractors are as fastidious with tax and NIC payments as they might be and their problems tend to become their agent's problems. By employing contractors only on a limited company basis, whereby the contractor has to look after his own payments, the agent is able to distance himself from their difficulties.

3. To protect the agent from liability. When an agent directly employs a contractor on PAYE, the agency assumes liability for that individual, his work and his conduct. By employing

a contractor's limited company, liability passes to that company.

## The advantages of owning a limited company

Although it may seem a nuisance having to own and administer a limited company just to obtain work and make life easier for the agent, there are advantages for the contractor:

- Unlike a PAYE contractor, your limited company will be paid the full hourly rate with no deductions at source. Your accountant will be able to manipulate this to your benefit, balancing income, expenses, tax and NIC to your advantage.

- Your company's registered office (at your accountant's address, see Form 228 below) will be located within the jurisdiction of an Inland Revenue office with whom your accountant is familiar and has constant, personal dealings. If your accountant's office is situated close to your home, your personal tax and company tax affairs will probably fall under the same tax office, thus concentrating much of your business administration in the smallest possible area.

- When you operate as a limited company instead of PAYE, you remove the need for your accountant to deal with your agent as your employer and the agent's area tax office, thus simplifying the management of your affairs.

## Obtaining a limited company

Before you proceed you should decide, in concert with your accountant, whether you need a UK based or an offshore company. If you intend to confine your contracting to the UK, then a UK based company will meet all your needs. UK companies are cheap to acquire: £75–£250.

If you will be working abroad, advantage must lie with an offshore company (see below, Tax and Social Security) although it will cost rather more to acquire: £250–£1,000.

There are two ways of acquiring a limited company, whether UK or offshore:

1. Form one from scratch. This method is not recommended as it tends to be expensive, time consuming and offers no particular advantage.

2. Buy one off-the-shelf. This method is quicker and cheaper than forming one from scratch because the company already exists, possibly having ceased trading. Firms that trade in such companies advertise in the *Exchange & Mart*, or your accountant will locate a company for you. A disadvantage of this method is that unless you want to spend time and money in changing the name of your off-the-shelf company, you will have to put up with the name it comes with.

Whichever of the two methods you use, it is better to let your accountant handle the actual acquisition for you. Although he will charge you for his work in buying and setting up your company, he will at least be in the picture right from the outset. This will make his job easier in the long run than having to pick up the threads of something that you have started yourself. The simpler his task is, the less his services are going to cost you.

> *Note:* There are specialists who provide complete financial services for contractors, including company acquisition (UK and offshore) and management, accountancy, VAT, payroll, pensions, insurance, etc. (see Appendix I). If you decide to employ such a specialist, be careful that you don't end up with a lot more services than you actually require.

If you require an offshore company, it can still be based within the British Isles. The Channel Islands and the Isle of Man are regarded as 'offshore' by the UK authorities, while some contractors favour the Irish Republic. There is no need to seek a base in some far flung island in the Caribbean or Pacific. The closer to home, the better.

### Dealing with the paper work

When you buy your company, whether onshore or offshore, a number of forms will arrive from the vendor of your company. The forms and their purposes will generally be:

● Notice of change of directors or secretaries or in their particulars.

● Notice of change in situation of registered office. Do not use your private address as your company registered office because if you sell your house and thus your registered office, you may become liable for capital gains tax. Seek your accountant's agreement to use his office address instead.

● Notice of accounting reference date, stating the date to which your company's accounts will be prepared.

● Return of allotments of shares issued for cash, detailing the company share issue. The share issue will cost about £100.

Your accountant will explain the forms to you. When you have signed them and they have been despatched, the vendor's fee paid and the paper work processed, your accountant will receive your company's Memorandum and Articles of Association and your Certificate of Incorporation of a Private Limited Company. You must send a copy of the Certificate to your agent. Be certain to give the agent's name and address to your accountant. The whole business of acquiring a company will only take a few days.

## Drawing up a contract between yourself and your limited company

Depending on the circumstances of your contract, your accountant may suggest that you draw up a further contract, this time between yourself and your limited company. The purpose of this is to determine:

● your position as an employee of your company

● the salary that your company will pay you

● company dividends payable to you

● NIC liabilities

● out of pocket expenses for which your company will reimburse you.

Having a contract between yourself and your company can make life a lot easier when and if you ever have to haggle with the tax man. Your solicitor, in conjunction with your accountant, will draw up such a contract for you according to your individual requirements.

## Opening a company bank account

You will also need to open a bank account for your company into which your company's income will be paid. Give your agent full details of the account, i.e. name, address and reference number of bank; name and number of company account, so that he will know where to send your money. Note that even if your income is ultimately destined for your private account, it must pass through the company account first.

## Coping with VAT

If your company operates in the UK and has an annual turnover of £47,000 plus, it must be registered for VAT. This means more boring bureaucracy but at least enables you to reclaim the VAT that your company has paid out. Your accountant will guide you in the completion of quarterly VAT returns.

If your company's registered office is also that of your accountant, the VAT man will go there if he needs to call, rather than to your home address. He will then be able to deal directly with your accountant, useful if you happen to be away.

## Administering your company

Once your company is formed and the money begins to flow, your duties as a company director are minimal and your accountant will advise you as matters proceed. Your most onerous task will be the minor, daily nuisance of keeping your records up to date and in order (see below, Keeping Accounts). There will also be a few short meetings with your accountant each year.

## Avoiding a limited company altogether

Many contractors ask whether this is possible and the short answer is 'yes'. There are specialists who provide 'shell' companies for contractors who are required to operate as, but do not wish to form their own limited companies (see Appendix III). In general, the contractor becomes a nominal employee of the shell company (often located offshore) which then issues invoices to the agency and charges the contractor 5 per cent plus for the service. The service is sometimes called networking.

## Question and answer session

Q. *If I form a limited company for my first contract, and then find that I don't need it for a subsequent assignment, do I have to close the company down?*

A.  No, just put your company on ice, i.e. ask your accountant to inform the Inland Revenue that the company has ceased trading for a period. It costs money to close down a company and you will be certain to need it again in the future.

Q.  *If I operate my limited company abroad, does it still have to be VAT registered?*
A.  In theory, yes, although scientific and technical services performed overseas are VAT zero rated. To get around the nonsense of charging your agent o per cent VAT, ask your accountant to apply to the Customs and Excise for a waiver.

Q.  *Networking seems rather attractive as I really don't want the bother of running my own company. Are there disadvantages?*
A.  Yes. While networking is tempting, it can lead to complications. The DSS and the Inland Revenue tend to take a dim view of the system and there can be problems in offsetting your expenses against tax. Investigate networking by all means but be guided by your accountant.

## KEEPING ACCOUNTS

When you have obtained a contract, established your limited company (where required) and chosen your accountant, you will need to keep a running record of your income and expenditure. Your accountant will need these records to ensure that you pay no more tax than is absolutely necessary.

### Don't put it off
Keeping accounts is not difficult as long as you start from the beginning of your contract and continue on a daily basis. Put off until tomorrow, accounting has a habit of getting left until it has grown into a monster that you can't bear to face, by which time your accountant is pleading for information and the Inland Revenue is breathing down your neck.

### The annual audit
If you operate as a limited company you will be required to submit your company accounts annually to Companies House. Before the budget of late 1993, company accounts had to be audited and submitted by a chartered accountant. The budget removed the

statutory audit for small companies with an annual turnover of less than £90,000. Theoretically at least, you can now prepare and submit your own accounts. However, since you will still need an accountant for all other aspects of your financial management, you might as well let him do the annual accounts as well, particularly if you are likely to be abroad when they are required.

### Recording cash flow

Before your contract begins you must obtain a cash book in which you can record the details of expenditure and income throughout the course of your contract, i.e.:

- the amount of each expenditure
- the date
- the nature of the expense
- VAT paid where applicable
- total expenditure per month
- total income per same month.

Number each expenditure entry consecutively from the beginning of the contract until the end. Keep all receipts, however minor, and write the number of the corresponding entry on the receipt. This will make it much easier for your accountant to match receipts with recorded entries. Ask for VAT receipts where applicable.

Keep a column in the cash book for explanatory notes against each entry. If you are working abroad remember that many of your receipts will be written in a foreign language that will probably be meaningless to your accountant, to the Inland Revenue and possibly to yourself at a later date when you try to remember what you spent and where and why you spent it.

Write the number of any cheques issued in the notes column and show from which account the cheque was drawn, whether personal, company or foreign.

When dealing with foreign currencies, note the prevailing exchange rate for all currencies concerned against the pound sterling for the month in question.

File all bank statements and other documents carefully as your accountant will need to see these. Keep copies of everything that you send to your accountant and note the date on which it was sent.

*Note:* If you are working abroad and become eligible for the

# Invoice

31/3/ 19 96

From SUPERCONTRACTOR LTD, 28 HIGH ST,
WESTCHESTER, BRISTOL BS95 9ZZ

To RENT-A-WHIZZ LTD, INDUSTRY HOUSE,
CAVERN ST, LIVERPOOL L105 5YZ, U.K.

| | £ | |
|---|---|---|
| RE-SERVICES TO UNFALL AVIATION GMBH, MUNICH, GERMANY 1/3/94 TO 31/3/94 220 HRS @ £35.00 P.H. | 7,700 | 00 |
| VAT ZERO RATED FOR SCIENTIFIC & TECHNICAL SERVICES O'SEAS. | | |
| TOTAL | 7,700 | 00 |

Fig. 9. Sample invoice for overseas contract.

# Invoice

97
............................ 20|3|. 19 9X

From. SUPERCONTRACTOR LTD., 28 HIGH ST.,
......... WESTCHESTER., BRISTOL BS95 9ZZ.

To .RENT-A-WHIZZ LTD., INDUSTRY HOUSE,
..... CAVERN ST., LIVERPOOL L105 5YZ..

| | | £ | |
|---|---|---|---|
| RE-SERVICES TO PCB ELECTRONICS LTD SIMWORTH, DERBY W/E 20/3/94 39 HOURS @ $27·00 P.H. | | 1,053 | 00 |
| PLUS VAT @ 17·5% | | 184 | 25 |
| TOTAL | | 1,237 | 27 |

Fig. 10. Sample invoice for UK contract.

### INTERNATIONAL CONSULTANTS LTD
### PROFIT AND LOSS ACCOUNT
### YEAR ENDED 31 MARCH 199X

|  | Note | 199X £ |
|---|---|---|
| TURNOVER |  | 70,000 |
| Net operating expenses | 1 | 69,000 |
| PROFIT ON ORDINARY ACTIVITIES BEFORE TAXATION |  | 241 |
| Tax on profit on ordinary activities |  | 60 |
| RETAINED PROFIT FOR THE FINANCIAL YEAR |  | 181 |

### NOTES TO THE ACCOUNTS

1. NET OPERATING EXPENSES

| | |
|---|---|
| Directors' remuneration | 54,500 |
| Employer's NIC | 5,559 |
| Travel expenses | 1,500 |
| Accommodation and subsistence | 7,000 |
| Accountancy | 1,000 |
| Insurance | 200 |
| | 69,000 |

Fig. 11. Extract from sample company annual accounts.

100 per cent tax reduction after one year (see below, Applying the One Sixth Rule), you will not be able to offset your expenses against tax because you won't be paying tax in the first place. Keep records all the same, in case you do not become eligible.

## Taking extra care with travel tickets

Take particular care of air and sea travel tickets. You may need these to prove that you were not in the UK at certain times if you are claiming the 100 per cent income tax reduction.

When recording the purchase of tickets bought several weeks ahead of their actual use, enter the dates of purchase and the dates of the journeys for which the tickets were bought. Retrospective matching of tickets with receipts and entries can be difficult when purchase and use dates do not match and may not be entirely legible on the ticket.

## Invoicing your agent

If you are operating as a limited company, you will need to submit a monthly invoice to your agent (see Figs. 9 and 10). For this you will require a duplicate invoice book. When you submit an invoice, note the number of the invoice, the date and the amount in a space reserved for 'income' in your cash book.

*Notes to Fig. 11:* Accounts based on a Type 4 Overseas contract (see Tax and Social Security) i.e. contractor is employee of his own UK based limited company.

During the year the contractor has worked 1,750 hours @ £40 per hour, therefore his company has earned £70,000 shown as turnover.

The company as employer pays Class 1 NIC for the first year of the contract, as above. The contractor must pay Class 1 NIC from his salary, i.e. director's remuneration £54,500.

No income tax is payable as the contractor is entitled to the 100 per cent reduction (see Applying the One Sixth Rule).

'Tax on profit on ordinary activities £60' is Corporation Tax.

## UNDERSTANDING TAX AND SOCIAL SECURITY

The great attraction of contracting is that of earning large sums of money. High earnings unfortunately, attract high rates of income tax and for the limited company contractor, employer's Class I NIC and possibly corporation tax.

## Being prepared

Wherever your contract is located you must ascertain at the outset your obligations regarding tax and social security. Confusion and trouble can follow if you do not. If you are responsible for making your own payments, ask your accountant to determine how much money you should set by to meet them.

Ignoring your obligations makes financial planning in other areas futile if it is likely to be suddenly disrupted by pressing demands from the Inland Revenue, the DSS or a foreign authority. More than a few contractors have been rudely shocked out of their fool's paradise to find themselves not comfortably wealthy but seriously in deficit.

Fig. 12 shows the tax and social security position applicable to the contract types identified at the beginning of this chapter.

You will see from Fig. 12. that contractors operating abroad through offshore companies are the most favoured as, in addition to the possibility (shared with other types of contract) of a 100 per cent tax reduction, they have no liability for Class 1 contributions and may pay the Class 3 contribution from the beginning of their foreign employment. This alone can save several thousand pounds.

> *Note:* You can use an offshore company in the UK but will still have to pay the full Class 1 NIC as for a UK company.

If you are employed abroad on a PAYE basis, UK income tax will be deducted at source by your agent but may be reclaimed if you become eligible for the 100 per cent reduction (see below, Applying the One Sixth Rule). Urge your agent to apply to the Inland Revenue for an NT (No Tax) coding for you as soon as possible. This may not be issued until the end of the current tax year, but at least means that there will be no further tax deductions for following years of the same contract.

Contractors working abroad through UK based or offshore limited companies have the advantage that there are no tax deductions at source, but should still ensure, through their accountants, that their personal NT status is established as early as possible. Note that tax will become payable if the contract lasts for less than a year (see below, Applying the One Sixth Rule).

Note that if you return to the UK at the end of a foreign contract,

**1. UK contract**

- Contractor hired by UK agent on PAYE basis.
- Agent pays employer's Class 1 NIC.
- Agent deducts income tax and employee's Class 1 NIC.

**2. UK contract**

- Contractor's own limited company hired by UK agent.
- Contractor is employee of his own company.
- Contractor's company pays employer's Class 1 NIC.
- Contractor pays employee's Class 1 NIC.
- Contractor pays employee's income tax.
- Contractor's company pays corporation tax if applicable.

**3. Overseas contract**

- Contractor hired by agent on PAYE basis.
- Agent pays employer's Class 1 NIC for first year of foreign employment only; not required thereafter.
- Agent deducts contractor's employee's Class 1 NIC for first year of foreign employment only, thereafter deducts Class 3 flat rate to preserve contractor's pension rights.
- Agent deducts contractor's UK income tax; tax free status possible under one sixth rule.

**4. Overseas contract**

- Contractor's own UK based limited company hired by UK agent.
- Contractor is employee of his own company.
- Contractor's company pays employer's Class 1 NIC for first year of foreign employment; not required thereafter.
- Contractor pays employee's Class 1 NIC for first year of foreign employment only; thereafter contractor pays own Class 3 flat rate NIC to preserve pension rights.
- Contractor pays employee's UK income tax; tax free

Fig. 12. Tax and social security by contract type.

**5. Overseas contract**
- Contractor's own offshore limited company hired by UK agent.
- Contractor is employee of his own company.
- Contractor's offshore company not required to pay employer's Class 1 NIC for first year of foreign employment and no requirement thereafter.
- Contractor not required to pay employer's Class 1 NIC during first year of foreign employment and no requirement thereafter.

**6. Overseas contract**
- Contractor hired by agent on PAYE basis.
- Agent pays employer's Class 1 NIC for first year of foreign employment only.
- Agent deducts contractor's employee's Class 1 NIC for first year of foreign employment only, thereafter contractor becomes contributor to local social security scheme under host country/UK reciprocal agreement.
- Agent deducts contractor's UK income tax. Contractor may be required to pay local income tax after stated period.

**7. Overseas contract**
- Contractor hired by UK or foreign agent.
- Contractor pays local income tax and social security contributions from commencement of contract.

work in the UK for a while and then go abroad again, the first year of full Class 1 payments begins again.

*Note:* See Arranging Social Security, Medical and Other Insurance for applicability of UK Social Security abroad.

## Paying tax abroad
If you do fall into the local tax net whilst contracting abroad, make sure that you obtain official confirmation from the foreign tax authority that you have paid tax during your employment in the

country concerned in order to avoid being taxed on the same earnings again when you return to the UK. Pay slips showing tax deducted whilst abroad will probably not be regarded as sufficient evidence for this purpose. Contact your local Inland Revenue office for details of taxation agreements between the UK and your destination country.

Tax matters abroad tend to be complex and official forms make British tax forms look simple by comparison. In some continental countries the forms are so complicated that a special breed of professional fillers-in of tax forms exists.

The longer a PAYE contractor remains in his host country, the greater the likelihood that he will eventually have to regularise his position as far as local taxation and social security is concerned.

## Question and answer session

Q. *How and when do I make payments for tax and social security?*

A. Your accountant will calculate the amounts when they fall due and will request a cheque from you for forwarding to the Inland Revenue.

Q. *I am going to work abroad and have been told by my agent that my contract salary will be split. A small portion will be payable in my host country and will be tax liable there. Will I be taxed on the remainder remitted to the UK.*

A. The amount payed into the UK (or anywhere that you choose) will be tax free in the UK if you are able to ob- serve the one sixth rule (see below, Applying the One Sixth Rule).

## APPLYING THE ONE SIXTH RULE

The one sixth rule and the 100 per cent reduction of UK taxation on money earned abroad are widely discussed, quoted, queried and misunderstood aspects of contracting. Confused contractors debate the matter endlessly. Available documentation on the subject is often so difficult to understand that it compounds the confusion. Even some accountants are puzzled by the situation, which is reason in itself to choose an accountant familiar with the regulations applying to people who work abroad.

Current tax and NIC rates (1996–7) for the UK are:


### Income tax
20% on earnings up to £3900 p.a.
24% on earnings up to £25,500 p.a. and 40% thereafter.
(Personal allowances are £3765 p.a. plus £1790 p.a. [relief restricted to 15%] married couple's allowance).

### Class 1 NIC
Employer       —not contracted out
                    10.2% (10% after 6.4.97)
                    —contracted out
                    10.2% on first 61 p.w.; 7.2% to £455 p.w.;
                    10.2% over £455 p.w.

Employee       —not contracted out
                    2% on first £61 p.w.
                    10% on remainder up to £455 p.w.
                    —contracted out
                    2% on first £61 p.w.
                    8.2% on remainder up to £455 p.w.
                    —over £455, no additional contributions
                    payable.

### Class 3 NIC
£5.95 per week

### Corporation tax
25% on small companies with profit limit of up to £300,000.


*Note:* The figures above are liable to periodic revision.

Fig. 13. Tax and NIC rates 1996–97.

## Understanding the rule

Basically, you may qualify for a 100 per cent reduction (or deduction) of UK income tax on earnings from overseas employment as long as:

● The work is carried out wholly or partly outside the UK for at least one year (365 days).

● Visits made to the UK during that year do not exceed 62 consecutive days or a total period not greater than one sixth of that year.

Note that one sixth of 365 is 60.83, not 62. Always calculate on the lower figure to be on the safe side. If you break the one sixth rule, you will not quality for the 100 per cent reduction.

## Home visits

It is on the question of visits to the UK that the greatest confusion arises, particularly with planning whether you should be at home or abroad at a particular time in respect of the one sixth rule and your qualification for the 100 per reduction.

The main point to remember is that one sixth means just that. Whether your time in the UK is spent as one long period or several smaller ones, that time, expressed as days, must never exceed one sixth of that abroad–home–abroad total. The example in Fig. 14 illustrates the point.

The final fraction gives an amount less than one sixth, i.e. less than one sixth of the 365 days has been spent in the UK, therefore the 100 per cent reduction applies. If more than 62 days had been spent in the UK, the final fraction would have been greater than one sixth and the 100 per cent reduction would not have applied.

The foregoing is a simple example because only one visit to the UK was made during the year. Adding A, B and C together forms what the Inland Revenue call a 'Single Qualifying Period'.

When more than one visit (B1, B2, B3 etc.) to the UK are made, each subsequent period abroad (C1, C2, C3 etc.) is a further Relevant Period. By adding further UK visits (Bs) and periods abroad (Cs) to the calculation, the Single Qualifying Period is continuously extended to the end of the last full day of each (relevant C, C1, C2, C3, C4) period abroad.

*Key to example:*

A      = first spell abroad (Qualifying Period in Inland
           Revenue jargon)
B      = first visit to the UK
C      = second spell abroad (Relevant Period)
B1    = second visit to UK
C1    = third spell abroad (second Relevant Period)

## Example: One UK visit during first year

A      = 180 days
B      = 45 days
C      = 140 days

To calculate the 'one sixth':

$$\frac{B\ (45\ \text{days})}{A\ (180\ \text{days})\ +\ B\ (45\ \text{days})\ +\ C\ (140\ \text{days})} = \frac{45}{365} = \frac{1}{8.11}$$

Fig. 14. Example of one sixth calculation.

## The rolling one sixth

The point to remember is that the one sixth is a rolling figure and must be constantly maintained. It is not so much the length of each UK visit that counts but the length of the following Qualifying Period abroad. If you break the one sixth by coming home too early, you cannot make it up by staying abroad longer the next time, even if at the end of the year you still have a total of less than 60 days spent in the UK.

## Projecting the calculation

In practice this means that you must project the calculation ahead and plan your visits to the UK so that your last day of each Relevant Period abroad falls within the one sixth and you can come home without jeopardising your qualification for the 100 per cent reduction.

   The best way to achieve this is to construct a ready reckoner chart, or adapt a calendar, showing the days numbered from Day

1, the day of your initial departure from the UK onwards. The chart can be extended indefinitely throughout the duration of the contract. Fig. 15 shows a sample, partial chart.

In the case illustrated, the day of departure from the UK was 20 January. This becomes Day 1 on the chart. Days 1 to 16 inclusively form A, the Qualifying Period.

Days 17 to 23 inclusively form B, the first UK visit. Note that Day 17 (5 February) is the day of travel, days of arrival in the UK being counted as days in the UK and therefore part of B. It is where you are at midnight that counts.

Days 24 to 51 inclusively, the second spell abroad, form C, the first Relevant Period. Note that Day 24 (12 February), the day of departure from the UK, is counted as a day abroad.

A + B + C form the Single Qualifying Period. Days 52 to 60 inclusively form B1, the second UK visit, while Days 61 to 96 inclusively form C1, the second Relevant Period, i.e. the third spell abroad.

A + B + C + B1 + C1 extend the Single Qualifying Period and so on. Continuing thus for 365 days would ensure qualification for the 100 per cent reduction.

If you are getting confused at this stage by all the jargon, don't worry! The officialese is included here simply because it is used by the Revenue and one has to defer to the system in order to understand it. Once learned and understood, you can quietly ignore the gobbledy-gook and concentrate on applying the rules to your benefit.

## Planning ahead

The trick in maintaining continuity of the Single Qualifying Period lies in not coming home to the UK too soon and thereby breaking the one sixth rule.

A contractor observing the schedule illustrated uses the chart to plan ahead and calculate the minimum length of time that he must remain abroad after each UK visit. All that he has to do is to count the days at home in the UK column and to multiply the last full day by 6. The result at the end of the first visit, 6 x 7 = 42, shows that he must then stay abroad until the end of Day 42. 42 ÷ 7 = 6 and this is entered against Day 42 in the 1/6 column. The earliest day that the contractor can return to the UK without breaking the one sixth is thus Day 43, marked with *.

In the case shown, the contractor did not choose to make a second visit to the UK until Day 52, remaining in the UK until

| DATE | JAN DAY | UK | 1/6 | FEB DAY | UK | 1/6 | MAR DAY | UK | 1/6 | APR DAY | UK | 1/6 |
|---|---|---|---|---|---|---|---|---|---|---|---|---|
| 1 | | : | : | 13 : | | : | 41 : | | : | 72 : | | : |
| 2 | | : | : | 14 : | | : | 42 : | ÷7 | 6.0 | 73 : | | : |
| 3 | | : | : | 15 : | | : | 43 : | ★ | : | 74 : | | : |
| 4 | | : | : | 16 : | | : | 44 : | | : | 75 : | | : |
| 5 | | : | : | 17 : | 1 | B | 45 : | | : | 76 : | | : |
| 6 | | : | : | 18 : | 2 | : | 46 : | | : | 77 : | | : |
| 7 | | : | : | 19 : | 3 | : | 47 : | | : | 78 : | | : |
| 8 | | : | : | 20 : | 4 | : | 48 : | | : | 79 : | | : |
| 9 | | : | : | 21 : | 5 | : | 49 : | | : | 80 : | | : |
| 10 | | : | : | 22 : | 6 | : | 50 : | | : | 81 | | : |
| 11 | | : | : | 23 : | 6x7 | =42 | 51 : | | : | 82 | | : |
| 12 | | : | : | 24 : | | C | 52 : | 8 | B1 | 83 | | : |
| 13 | | : | : | 25 : | | : | 53 : | 9 | : | 84 | | : |
| 14 | | : | : | 26 : | | : | 54 : | 10 | : | 85 | | : |
| 15 | | : | : | 27 : | | : | 55 : | 11 | : | 86 | | : |
| 16 | | : | : | 28 : | | : | 56 : | 12 | : | 87 | | : |
| 17 | | : | : | 29 : | | : | 57 : | 13 | : | 88 | | : |
| 18 | | : | : | 30 : | | : | 58 : | 14 | : | 89 | | : |
| 19 | | : | : | 31 : | | : | 59 : | 15 | : | 90 | | : |
| 20 | 1 : | | A | 32 : | | : | 60 : | 6x16 | =96 | 91 | | : |
| 21 | 2 : | | : | 33 : | | : | 61 : | | C1 | 92 | | : |
| 22 | 3 : | | : | 34 : | | : | 62 : | | : | 93 | | : |
| 23 | 4 : | | : | 35 : | | : | 63 : | | : | 94 | | : |
| 24 | 5 : | | : | 36 : | | : | 64 : | | : | 95 | | : |
| 25 | 6 : | | : | 37 : | | : | 65 : | | : | 96 : | ÷16 | 6.0 |
| 26 | 7 : | | : | 38 : | | : | 66 : | | : | 97 : | ★ | : |
| 27 | 8 : | | : | 39 : | | : | 67 : | | : | 98 | | : |
| 28 | 9 : | | : | 40 : | | : | 68 : | | : | 99 | | : |
| 29 | 10 : | | : | XX : | | : | 69 : | | : | 100 | | : |
| 30 | 11 : | | : | XX : | | : | 70 : | | : | 101 : | | : |
| 31 | 12 : | | : | XX : | | : | 71 : | | : | XX : | | : |

Fig. 17. Sample one sixth projection.

his departure on Day 61. As his last full day (Day 60) in the UK was his 16th at home in total, he projects ahead by multiplying 16 by 6. The result, 96, tells him that he must remain abroad until at least the end of Day 96. He may not travel home again until Day 97 at the earliest. Note that the one sixth calculation is repeated against Day 96 and Day 97 is marked with ★.

Forward projections can thus be continued indefinitely. Remember that the longer each visit to the UK is, the longer your next Relevant Period abroad must be. You may have to 'save up' time if you are planning a long break in the UK or accept that once the visit is over, you will be stuck abroad until your one sixth is back in credit.

If you come home frequently:

- the use of such a chart is highly recommended

- it is all too easy to break the one sixth inadvertently if you do not keep a careful watch on your movements.

- forward projections are in any case essential when you are booking travel tickets several weeks in advance of your journey (see Travelling but Mostly Flying in Chapter 4).

If you are planning to draw up your own chart you can include any number of refinements to suit yourself but make sure that you have the correct number of days in each month and be careful of leap years.

### Getting your year in

Contractors often talk of 'getting their year in'. This simply means that they are looking forward to clearing their first year abroad, safe in the knowledge that even if they break the one sixth thereafter, they are eligible for the 100 per cent tax deduction for that first year.

Once the initial year (which does not have to coincide with a tax year) is safely completed, the rolling one sixth should be maintained. Failure to do so would render income earned after the initial year liable to taxation.

### Keeping records

At all times you must keep careful records of your visits to the UK and retain any receipts etc. that will help to prove that you were abroad at all other times. If the Inland Revenue decide to challenge the dates of your UK visits, the onus will be on you to verify your claims of absence.

### Non-residency

It is a common misconception that you have to establish non-UK resident status in order to qualify for the 100 per cent reduction. The fact of the matter is that you can remain a UK resident the whole time that you are abroad. All you have to do is to observe the one sixth rule with regard to your UK visits. An advantage of remaining a UK resident is that you can still claim your income tax allowances should this become necessary, e.g. if you do not get your year in and become liable to pay income tax.

## Exceptions

If it is clear from the outset of your contract that you are going to be taxed in the country of your employment, there is no advantage in observing the one sixth rule. You can come home as often as you wish but you must make sure that you can obtain proof that you are paying tax abroad. In these circumstances overseas earnings would be chargeable to UK income tax in full and credit given for the overseas tax already deducted.

## Keeping abreast of changes

Changes to the regulations regarding the one sixth rule are often proposed. Make sure that your accountant advises you of any changes. There is no point in being careful in your movements if you are going to be caught out by new rules of which you were unaware.

## Case history: A close shave with the one-sixth

Peter Bryant had been on contract in Austria for almost a year when his wife was taken ill and he had to spend a few weeks in England until she recovered. The anniversary of the beginning of his contract occurred while he was at home.

Peter was alarmed when his accountant told him that although he had only spent 58 days in the UK during the year, he would not be entitled to the 100% deduction because the year should have ended with Peter's being abroad in order to constitute a single qualifying period.

Peter's initial reaction was a sick feeling that in addition to his lost earnings, he would now be facing a hefty tax bill. His accountant pointed out that was not so because:

(i) the beginning of the qualifying period could effectively be moved to a later date than the the actual date of commencement of Peter's contract abroad.

(ii) as long as Peter remained abroad long enough to maintain his rolling one-sixth from the new date of commencement of the qualifying year, and was abroad when that year ended (longer if the contract lasted), the 100% deduction could still be applied to the whole of his contract except for the period from its actual commencement to the revised beginning of the qualifying period. And even to this period, Peter's personal allowances would apply, thus much reducing the amount of tax payable.

Greatly relieved, Peter returned to Austria.

### Question and answer session

Q. *If I break the one sixth, how would the Inland Revenue find out?*

A. You may be asked to supply a list of the dates of your UK visits. If the Inland Revenue decide to challenge these dates, the onus will be on you to verify your claims of absence. If doubts remain, checks on your movements could be made.

Q. *My contract abroad is expected to last rather less than a year. How can I get my year in to qualify for the 100 per cent reduction?*

A. This depends on how close to the year you will be at the end of your contract and how much time you have spent in the UK during its course. It may be worth the cost of remaining abroad after you finish working in order to obtain the reduction. This assumes of course, that you do not find another contract abroad fairly quickly.

## HANDLING THE MONEY

The ways in which a contractor handles his money is essentially a matter of personal choice and the dictates of circumstance. The following hints, directed mostly at the contractor working abroad, may be useful.

### In the beginning

The beginning of a contract can be an expensive time, with perhaps an additional car to buy and accommodation deposits to find. Some agents will arrange a loan to carry their contractors through their initial expenses.

### Payment

Different agents have different approaches to paying their contractors. Most will send your money to any destination that you· may choose. Others, less helpful, will insist that all the contractors in a particular site receive their payment into one branch of a local bank. This is to simplify the agent's task by having only one bank to deal with. This will then cost you the price of the transfer to move your money to the destination of your choice. If the arrangements that are offered do not suit you, try to get them changed.

## Splitting payments

Do not ask the agent to split your payments between two or more accounts. This increases the chances of confusion, makes it more difficult to keep track of your money and will attract additional transfer fees. Having more than one bank account also complicates matters when you come to prepare your accounts.

## Delayed payment

There can be problems if you arrive on a contract that has only just begun. It can take a while for the money to start flowing from the client to the agent. Under such circumstances the agent may be reluctant to pay his contractors until his own income is ensured. This does not happen very often but is not unknown.

## Meeting expenses

As most contracts will entail the contractor working away from home, he will have to make arrangements to ensure that he can meet his expenses.

Whilst working in the UK the contractor will probably come home every weekend and will be able to pay his bills by cheque or credit card and will only need to carry enough money for incidental expenses. It is most unlikely that he will even need to open a bank account local to his place of work.

When working abroad however, the contractor will need to consider other methods of handling cash.

## Foreign bank accounts

Many contractors open bank accounts in their country of employment and in some cases this will be unavoidable. A disadvantage of this is that foreign bank accounts mean official documents with your name upon them. Continental current accounts are usually interest bearing, tax liable and therefore notifiable to the local tax authorities. While your position in the foreign country might and should be completely legal, it is never good policy to give officialdom reason to ask questions. Bank statements written in a foreign language will also confuse your accountant. Wherever possible, avoid establishing a foreign bank account and meet your expenses from your UK acount.

## Managing without a foreign bank account

If you decide to manage without a bank account abroad, the following will give you access to money, all drawn on your UK account.

### Traveller's cheques

These are a useful means of carrying money with security but have the disadvantage of having to be paid for at the time of purchase. This is money that could be earning you interest, spent ahead of the actual expenditure.

In the early stages of a contract however, it is a good idea to take a minimum of £500 in travellers cheques with you to help meet initial expenses (even if you intend to open an account abroad) but not to rely on them in the long run.

Travellers cheques may be cashed at many hotels and railway stations, but expect to pay a higher commission than at a bank.

Many UK banks can issue sterling travellers cheques over the counter, but if your local branch is small or if you require cheques in the currency of your destination country, you may have to order a few days in advance.

### Eurocheques

More flexible than travellers cheques are Eurocheques issued by your UK bank in booklets of ten and accompanied by a plastic identity card. Eurocheques can be cashed in any European country and in some countries in north Africa (in any local currency) or used to pay for goods and services. Look for the Eurocheque sign.

Eurocheques may be cashed to any amount (just like a normal cheque) up to the permitted maximum. This is usually the equivalent of about £100 per cheque. More than one cheque may be cashed at a time but three or more may be refused or require further personal identification. Order your Eurocheques as far in advance of your departure as possible.

If you use Eurocheques, don't wait until the last cheques are used before you order more. There is a re-order form in the booklet. Allow plenty of time for the re-order to be processed and for the cheques to reach you. If you are travelling home regularly, it is probably better to have the cheques sent to your home address than to your address abroad because continental postal systems are much slower than in the UK.

## Credit card

Most major British credit cards are recognised abroad and can be used, as at home, to draw cash or to pay for goods and services. Settle credit card bills as soon as possible to avoid payment of interest.

*Note:* Visa cards may not be recognised in Germany.

## Bank transfer

This is a useful method to cover major expenses such as rent. Monthly sums can be paid straight into your landlord's account. Warn your bank in advance of your departure that you may want to transfer money abroad and seek their advice as to the best method for your anticipated purposes.

### Saving against a rainy day

As a contractor you must always keep enough money behind you to see you through any period of unemployment. Whatever your financial aspirations and current obligations, create a rainy day fund as soon as you can. £10,000 is a suggested amount. Keep it where it will earn interest for you but will be accessible in times of need. Ask your accountant and bank for advice. Do not regard your rainy day fund as part of any subsequent investment.

### Investing for the future

A contract income over a prolonged period can make many things possible. You may wish to pay off your mortgage, buy other property, start a business or simply to retire early. However your future begins to take shape, remember the following:

● Obtain the widest advice available regarding investment under prevailing conditions.

● All investment contains an element of risk. The greater the potential reward, the higher the risk will be.

● Never enter into any agreement without discussing it with your accountant first.

● Above all, *never* undertake any financial commitment that can only be serviced by a contract salary.

## Case history: when ambition overtakes caution

During the late 1980s, Ivor Davies was working in Germany on a contract that seemed set to last for several years. Looking for an investment that would provide a healthy profit, he became interested in rapidly rising property values in the UK. Although he could not afford to buy outright he discovered, in the heady financial climate of the time, that there were several banks and finance houses who were impressed by his high earnings and only too willing to lend him money for deposits. Ivor was thus able to buy three houses which he rented out.

It was not long however, before Ivor fell victim to the bust that followed the boom. Firstly, interest rates rose so rapidly that the rents he received from his properties failed to cover his mortgage repayments. Secondly, two of his tenants were made redundant and were unable to pay their rents or find other accommodation and thus became squatters whom Ivor found impossible to evict. The third and final blow came when the end of the Cold War caused the cancellation of the defence related project on which Ivor was employed.

With no contract income, Ivor's debts mounted. When he did finally regain repossession of his houses, he was forced to sell them for far less than their original purchase values. Even when Ivor found another contract, his income barely covered the accumulated interest payments that he had incurred. Ivor found that he had fallen into the classic contract trap; he needed a contract salary, not to get ahead of the game but just to keep his head above water.

## Bringing the money home

When you leave a foreign assignment, make sure that you bring all your money home with you. If you have had to open a foreign bank account, close it and withdraw or transfer all funds before you leave the country in question. If you have paid a deposit on accommodation, get it back before you come home. It can be quite difficult to get money out of people when you are no longer around in person.

With care, planning and the willpower to prevent your expenditure from matching your income, you will soon begin to see the financial rewards that contracting can bring.

## Question and answer session

Q.  *Can I use a British bank card in foreign cash dispensers?*
A.  In many parts of the world, notably Europe, British cards can

be used in 'hole in the wall' cash dispensers. Check applicability with your bank.

Q. *Can I cash UK cheques abroad?*
A. In some circumstances this is possible with the prior agreement of the banks concerned. You will almost certainly need written authority from your UK bank and if you are bound for non-English speaking parts, it is recommended that you obtain a translation of the authority. Again, enquire at your bank, preferably well in advance of your departure.

Q. *I have heard that some contracts are paid in foreign currency. What happens when the contract is located in a country that restricts the export of its currency.*
A. Generally, you will be paid from outside that country in a currency other than that of the host country. Contractors working in South Africa for example, are often paid in Swiss francs. You are normally allowed to re-export any funds that you have originally imported into a restricted country.

## CHECKLIST

1. Are you clear about the type of contract for which you are negotiating (PAYE, limited company, etc.) and the administrative responsibilities you will incur?
2. If a limited company is required, is everything organised?
3. Do you have a cash book for recording expenditure and income?
4. Have you obtained an invoice book?
5. Are you certain of the tax and social security obligations of your contract?
6. Have you understood the application of the one sixth rule?
7. Have you made arrangements for handling expenditure and income?

# 4
# Going on Contract

Starting a new job is always a significant event. Beginning a contract can mean a total upheaval and readjustment of your lifestyle unless you are fortunate enough to find a contract within commuting distance of your home. Careful preparation and a degree of foreknowledge will ease that readjustment.

This chapter deals with:

- medical cover
- what you should take with you
- travelling to and from your contract location
- finding accommodation in the UK and abroad
- the contract team leader
- behaviour on contract

## ARRANGING SOCIAL SECURITY, MEDICAL AND OTHER INSURANCE

Contractors as a breed have a remarkable ability to stay healthy. The true contractor will come to work unless actually incapacitated by illness. Being hourly paid is a powerful incentive to not linger in bed with some trifling ailment that might keep a permanent employee with his paid sick leave at home.

It has often been said, amongst contractors at least, that if everybody were employed on a contract basis, time lost to industry through absenteeism would be drastically reduced. This is possibly true. A major manufacturer of aircraft in the West Country has a technical publications department employing one hundred people. At any one time 10 per cent of that hundred is off sick, or ostensibly so. The cost to that company is considerable. If they could replace their permanent staff with hourly paid contractors, the cost to the company of absenteeism would diminish sharply.

But even contractors are sometimes away from work through illness or accident, more usually the latter. When a contractor does not work he does not get paid. If he is abroad, he may also have to pay hefty medical bills unless he has taken appropriate precautions.

## Taking precautions

Before undertaking any contract abroad, ensure that you have sufficient cover against medical bills, hospitalisation and repatriation, through the DSS, EU member state arrangements, British reciprocal agreements with foreign countries or private insurance. Information can be obtained from:

The Department of Social Security
Overseas Branch
Newcastle-upon-Tyne NE98 1YX
Tel: (0191) 217 5000

The following DSS leaflets apply:

*NI 38 Social Security Abroad*
*SA 29 Your social security, insurance, benefits and health care rights in the European Union (EU)*

Further leaflets in the SA series provide information on reciprocal agreements applicable to countries outside the EU.

## Taking out private cover

It is in any case a good idea to take out private insurance against all misfortunes when working abroad, even within the EU. Some countries operate a 'pay now, claim later' system or insurance schemes that are partly state and partly privately administered. Proof that you can pay for services rendered may speed up their provision.

Visit your local insurance broker before you leave home and:

● tell him exactly what you will be doing and where you will be doing it

- ask for an insurance policy tailored to meet your personal requirements

- insist that the cover is taken out with a company expert in insuring people working abroad.

While you are talking to your insurance man, you may also wish to discuss other insurance, e.g. loss of earnings, loss of baggage, travel, etc. Do not put off arranging your insurance until it is too late.

### Case history: an expensive stay in hospital

Ray Taylor's contract in Rome was rudely interrupted when he made the mistake of expecting an Italian driver to stop for him as he crossed the road on a pedestrian crossing. Concussed and bruised, he spent several weeks in hospital before he discovered that the hospital was insisting on cash payment for his treatment, reciprocal arrangements notwithstanding. (This can happen in places where the bureaucracy only functions spasmodically.) As Ray had not taken out private insurance, he was presented with heavy hospital bills that he could not immediately pay. Ray's client company also refused to allow him to return to work until the hospital gave him a clean bill of health, something they would not do until their bill was paid despite all assurances that the matter was in hand. Eventually they stopped feeding him and then removed his clothes in case he absconded. It was left to Ray's fellow contractors to bring food parcels into the hospital for him.

The impasse was only resolved when the team leader gathered enough EU type paperwork to convince the hospital that the bills would be settled. Ray, having lost several weeks' income unnecessarily, vowed that next time he went on contract he would make certain that he took out private medical insurance before he left home.

### Question and answer session

Q. *If I go to work in an EU member state, how do I demonstrate that I am paying NIC in the UK?*

A. You should obtain Form E101 from the DSS Overseas Branch.

Q. *How much will private insurance cost?*

A. As a rough guide, variable according to personal circumstances, the premium for a policy covering most medical contingencies and repatriation will cost from £500 p.a. This sum represents a weekly expenditure of £10, or the price of a few beers, a very low outlay for peace of mind.

Q. *What other insurances should I take out?*
A. You should certainly insure your personal possessions against loss, theft and damage.

Q. *What about loss of earnings insurance?*
A. Loss of earnings insurance through illness/accident can be arranged with medical insurance. Insurance against unemployment is likely to be prohibitively expensive because of the very nature of contracting.

## TAKING THE KITCHEN SINK

When you reach the stage of actually setting out for a contract, you will inevitably wonder what you should take with you.

### Packing for the UK

If you are bound for an assignment in the UK you will have few problems because you will probably be travelling by car and will usually come home on Friday night and return on Monday morning. With so little time away and frequent home visits, you do not have to plan far ahead and can easily remedy mistakes. Essentials will include:

- Written instructions from agent about contract commencement (directions, timing, whom to report to, etc.).

- Copy of contract.

- Cash book.

- Copy of CV.

- Invoice book (for limited company contractors).

- Agency contact book.

- Money, credit cards, etc.

● Professional materials.

● Vehicle documentation and driving licence (don't be caught away from home without these in case you are stopped by the police and are required to produce them).

● Copy of birth certificate (may be required for security purposes).

● Clothing for one week.

● Toilet gear.

● Towels (usually provided in lodgings but not always).

● Personal medication including prescriptions (especially for spectacles).

● Large-scale map of destination city/region.

## Packing for overseas

If you are heading for the Continent (or further afield) you will need to plan more carefully when deciding what to take with you as you will probably be away from home for weeks on end and accordingly less able to amend omissions. It is also important not to go overboard by taking too many things with you; in the early stages of a foreign contract you may change lodgings several times before you find somewhere of your own (see below, Finding Accommodation). Until you settle, possessions are an encumbrance, even if you travel by car and are not limited, as with air travel, by the amount of baggage that you can carry.

   In addition to the items in the list above, and clothing for about three weeks, the following will be essential and/or useful:

● Passport (not visitor's passport, and not about to expire).

● Travel tickets.

● Money in its various forms.

● Vehicle documentation including Green card (see below, Taking Your Car Abroad).

- Personal insurances (see above, Arranging Medical Cover).

- Plenty of passport photographs (for foreign bureaucracy, e.g. permits, security, registration, etc.).

- Copies of birth/marriage Certificates (as above).

- Note of National Insurance number.

- Phrase book (see Learning the Language in Chapter 5).

- Pocket dictionary, English/applicable foreign language.

- A few good books (you may have time to kill).

- Small, powerful reading lamp with a long flex (lighting in Europe tends to be much dimmer than in Britain and hotel bedside lamps are often inadequately bright for prolonged reading).

- Portable radio capable of receiving the BBC.

- Small travelling iron.

- Universal electrical socket adaptor (obtainable from most electrical retailers and designed to fit the many different types of electrical socket found in Europe and to save you the trouble and expense of changing all your plugs).

- Packet of cold soak washing powder. Clothing left overnight in soak will be ready for rinsing in the morning. Many hotels do not object to the odd item being washed out. Hotel laundry services, where they exist, are expensive.

- Before you leave home compile a checklist of the things that you wish to take with you and cross each item off as it is packed.

- Make sure that all your luggage is labelled and that any that you will have to leave in lodgings is lockable.

## TRAVELLING BUT MOSTLY FLYING

Wherever your contract is located, you will wish to travel home as often as possible. Whether you regard it as a relaxing pleasure or an expensive bore, travel to and from your place of work requires a certain amount of planning. When arranging your journeys, always bear in mind that the cheapest form of travel is not necessarily the most cost effective, i.e. trains are much slower than aircraft and a few hours extra spent in the office will more than pay for the difference between a rail and an air ticket and your journey will be quicker and less tiring as a result.

### Travelling in the UK

Most contractors working in the UK use their own cars to travel to and from work and to journey home at weekends. The exception might be the contractor who lives at one end of the country and works at the other, in which case air travel becomes viable in terms of cost and time. The same guidelines apply to buying air tickets for travel within the UK as for foreign destinations (see below).

If you do elect to do all or most of your travelling by car, make sure that it is in good condition before your contract commences. A car that is normally used for short trips may develop faults when called upon to perform repeated long journeys at sustained high speeds. It will cost you a lot more than the price of a major service to be towed off the motorway and to lose time from the job.

When rail travel becomes a possibility, enquire about season/ reduced price tickets. If you are travelling any distance by rail and can be certain of catching a particular train, it is worth reserving a seat to avoid having to stand for the whole journey.

### Travelling to/from a foreign contract

Most contractors working on the continent fly out initially and then collect their cars on their first trip home (see below, Owning a Car Abroad). Thereafter they use their cars for transport to and from work and for journeys to the local airport for flights back to the UK. Driving home regularly means using car ferries which is time consuming and expensive. When planning flights, the following advice applies:

## Study the timetables

Obtain copies of timetables from travel agent or airline and make a list of all the departure and arrival times in your proposed itinerary (including rail or coach journeys at either end) and their alternatives should you be delayed.

## Plan for the one sixth

Always take the one sixth into account when planning trips home (see Applying the One Sixth Rule in Chapter 3).

## Book well in advance

London is a popular venue for vacationing Europeans. Flights to/from the Continent are often fully booked several weeks ahead, especially at holiday periods.

## Buy your tickets abroad

It is generally convenient to buy air tickets abroad, usually for the next flight that you plan to make and when you are already at the airport ready to fly home on a previously booked flight. This saves having to make a special trip to a travel agent during a crowded weekend at home.

## Allow plenty of time

When planning a journey, allow plenty of time at all stages, particularly when making connections. A delayed flight can mean a missed train. Give yourself adequate breathing space so that if you miss a coach or train it won't matter if you have to sit and wait for the next one. Having to rush for connections makes travelling an exhausting business.

## Familiarise yourself with the route to the airport

When you first arrive on a contract, it is worth making a dummy run to the airport to check how long the trip takes and to familiarise yourself with the route. Remember that you may be travelling alone and instructions given by helpful colleagues can suddenly become confusing when you are actually under way, particularly if there are diversions en route.

## Keep important things with you

Keep passport, tickets, boarding passes and money and car keys exactly where you know you can find them and preferably in an inside jacket pocket.

**Take hand luggage only**

Whenever possible, travel with hand luggage only. At most airports passengers carrying hand luggage only can check in at the departure gate. This saves possible lengthy queuing at the main check-in where more heavily laden passengers wait to have their baggage weighed. It makes sense anyway to travel as light as possible.

If you are forced to take a suitcase as well, try to carry important items in your hand luggage. Luggage carried in the hold of an aircraft can go astray and may take several days to catch up with you. This does not occur very often but it only needs to happen once for you to find out how inconvenient it can be to arrive on a contract without any shaving gear or at least a couple of changes of clothes.

Ensure that your hand luggage does not exceed the maximum weight permitted by the airline and stated on your air ticket. If your hand luggage looks heavy the airline may insist on its being sent in the aircraft's hold. This could mean that items you need for the flight are inaccessible to you unless you are quick witted enough to extract them from your overweight flight bag as it is taken from your care. If your passport happens to be in confiscated hand luggage you will cause yourself delays and inconvenience upon arrival.

**Always carry enough money**

At all times ensure that you have adequate funds to carry you through each country en route, particularly small change for telephones. An internationally recognised credit card is always useful but not all airports have facilities for making credit card telephone calls.

**Parking at an airport**

If you are parking your car at an airport, make a written note of the car park, floor and bay in which you have left your vehicle. It is all too easy to rely on memory and then find after a week or more at home that your car is not where you could have sworn you left it.

**Keep all receipts and tickets**

If you are operating as a limited company and are tax liable, travel expenses are tax deductible so retain evidence of the expenditure.

## Case history: more speed, less haste

Determined to maximise his earnings whilst on contract in Germany, Alec Daniels would remain in the office until the last moment that was compatible with catching the final flight to the UK on the day that he was going to leave.

On one occasion, pleased that he had managed to squeeze in another thirty minutes earning time, Alec began his high speed drive to the airport sixty miles away, making excellent time until his fanbelt broke and he had to spend half an hour fitting the spare. When he reached the airport the car park was full and he had to squeeze into the only space that he could find.

Alec's flight had already left. Although he managed to secure a first class seat on a delayed flight with another airline, he had to pay the full fare of several hundred pounds. The flight was late arriving at Heathrow and Alec was forced to hire a taxi in a vain attempt to catch the last train home from Reading. Finding his train gone, he had to take another taxi to his house a hundred miles away and at fearful cost.

Returning to Germany after the weekend, Alec scoured the airport car park for an hour before he gave up and reported his car stolen. It was quite safe, locked in the police pound for being parked on double yellow lines. After paying the statutory fine, Alec drove away reflecting on the dubious worth of his extra half an hour in the office.

## Question and answer session

Q. *Can I buy cheap rate air tickets?*

A. Apex or Super Apex tickets offer very substantial savings on air travel but you must book at least two weeks in advance of your flight. Your journeys must bracket a weekend period and tickets cannot be changed once purchased. Check all details on the ticket at the time of purchase.

Q. *Is it worth using charter flights?*

A. Charter flights often leave at unsocial hours from inconveniently situated airports and can be crowded and uncomfortable. In the holiday season they can be insufferable. If the airways are congested, charter flights will be delayed before scheduled flights.

## OWNING A CAR ABROAD

Unless you will be working and living in a city centre where car ownership is more nuisance than it is worth, you will almost certainly need a car when contracting abroad.

There are two approaches to car ownership overseas:

1. Buy a car in your host country.
2. Take your own car with you.

### Buying a car abroad

If at all possible, avoid this course of action as it can cause the following problems:

- Your name will appear on all manner of official documents which will alert minor officials to your presence, be it completely legal and above board, and may set in motion a chain of events that will drag you further and further into the system.

- When the contract ends you could find yourself with a left hand drive car that you may not wish to bring home. Left hand drive cars in Britain attract low prices and high insurance premiums. Even if you bring a right hand drive car back with you there are still the importation procedures to go through.

- If you decide to dispose of your foreign purchased car when your contract finishes, you will have all the problems of selling within an unfamiliar system plus that of needing transport up to the last moment. This usually means that you will have to get rid of your car in a hurry and at less than its real value.

There is certainly no advantage in buying a car abroad if you can take your own car with you. If distance, i.e. outside Europe prevents this, the above still applies. An alternative to buying locally is that of long term hire or leasing. Investigate the possibilities and balance the cost against the likely loss incurred through purchase and resale.

### Taking your own car abroad

With a British registered car you will have none of the above problems. Its right hand drive may attract glances but glances do not appear on official documents or carry date stamps. You will also have the advantage of being able to transport yourself and your belongings home at the end of the contract.

If you do take your own car abroad, the following must be considered:

### Condition

Make sure that your car is in a fit condition to travel long distances. Average speeds on the continent tend to be higher than in the UK and the general cut and thrust of European driving are wearing on car and driver. If you have any doubts about the fitness of your car to be taken abroad, leave it at home.

### Insurance

Make sure that your car is fully insured for use on the continent. Different insurance companies have different approaches to continental cover. Some issue policies that cover foreign travel at no extra cost while some will extend your cover by means of a Green Card or West European policy. Check with your insurance broker or company before you leave home.

### Documentation

Vehicle and driver documentation should be carried at all times. Although inspections at border posts are rare, you may be stopped by the police for a routine check. Most officials will not recognise a British MOT certificate, vehicle registration document, licence disc or insurance certificate when shown them but will be familiar with Green Cards and British driving licences. International Driving Licences (obtainable through the Automobile Association) are universally known and have the advantage of carrying the holder's photograph.

### Dead tax discs

While your car is abroad its tax disc or MOT certificate may well expire. These should be kept up to date even if it means bringing your car home to achieve this. A British tax disc may not be understood by continental officials, but an expired one in your windscreen will attract attention.

### Re-registration

If you intend keeping your car on the continent for any length of time, usually more than a year, local regulations will probably require that the car is re-registered in the host country. You cannot, or should not drive around on British plates indefinitely. This rule differs from country to country and is enforced with varying rigour.

### Roadside checks

In northern Europe roadside vehicle checks are fairly commonplace. The condition of tyres, lights and exhaust systems are the most common targets for inspection and on-the-spot fines are imposed for defective items. The rules are much more laxly enforced in southern Europe.

### Driving on the right

Driving on the right hand side of the road is not a problem, even if you have never done it before. Thinking about it is worse than actually doing it; you soon get used to it, although overtaking does require extra care. If you drive on the continent for any length of time you may have to make a conscious effort to remember to drive on the left when you return to the UK.

### Spare parts and servicing

As most cars are fairly universal these days and genuinely British cars almost non-existent, servicing and obtaining spare parts (except perhaps for some right hand drive steering components) for a 'British' car abroad is not a problem.

### Motorway tolls

Some European countries charge tolls for the use of their motorways. Ensure that you carry plenty of change at all times. It is not worth using minor roads to avoid paying tolls. Your journey will be slow and you run an increased risk of getting lost. In most countries tolls are payable at barriers erected across the motorways but in Switzerland you must buy a motorway pass or vignette. These cost thirty Swiss francs and are obtainable at border posts and garages. The vignette, valid for one year, must be displayed in the top, left hand corner of the windscreen. Do not be tempted to drive on Swiss motorways without a vignette. Spot checks are regularly made and offenders fined.

### Get ready for winter

European winters can be very severe, especially in the north. Ensure that your battery is in good condition and that there is sufficient anti-freeze in the car's cooling system to cope with local conditions. If in doubt, ask a garage to make a check. Carry snow chains or buy a set of winter tyres.

### Safety precautions

Do not drive on the Continent without a first aid kit or a warning triangle. In some countries you can be fined if you are found without either of these items. Ensure that your headlamps are changed for right hand dipping or adapted with stick on masks.

### Case history: a costly oversight with car insurance abroad

When Pete Simons went on contract to Italy he took his car with him and went in the belief that his third party insurance would provide the same cover in an EU country as it did in the UK. It wasn't until he had an accident, for which he was responsible, that he discovered that his insurance only provided the minimum cover required by law, i.e. he was covered for third party injuries but not for damage to other vehicles. He thus found himself with a heavy bill to pay for repairs to the vehicle that he had hit. Too late he realised that he should have (i) checked his insurance more carefully before he left home and (ii) extended his cover for use of his car abroad.

## FINDING ACCOMMODATION

When you arrive on site your first, overriding need will be somewhere to stay. In most cases initial accommodation will have been arranged either by the client company or if abroad, by the agent's representative on site, the Team Leader. Check the point with your agent before you leave home.

### Accommodation in the UK

Most contractors working in the UK, not wishing to incur the expense and responsibility of renting a flat that will be empty when they go home at weekends, either take bed and breakfast accommodation or rent a room with perhaps, use of a common kitchen.

If you are left, or prefer to find your own initial or subsequent accommodation you should consult:

- local newspapers
- parish magazines

- newsagents' advertisement boards
- the local library
- tourist information centres.

If you do decide to take a flat or bed-sit you will have to balance the likely length of the lease against the probable duration of your contract.

The minimum length of lease on a furnished flat is usually six months. You will have to pay one month's rent in advance and possibly a deposit as well. If you leave before your tenure has expired you may lose your deposit unless the flat is quickly re-let. You could offer to pay for the re-advertising of the flat if that will help protect your deposit.

A good alternative to a flat can be a caravan. Cheap to rent, or even to buy if you can find a site, a caravan can be just as comfortable as a flat and a lot less costly to keep warm.

### Sharing accommodation

If there are other contractors on site there may be some who have flats that they are willing to share. Many in fact will welcome the opportunity to reduce their own living expenses by splitting their costs with a colleague. Sharing should be approached with caution however, because the majority of shared accommodation situations do not endure in the long run. Working and living closely together simply results in people getting on each other's nerves.

### Accommodation abroad

Your foreign contract will almost certainly begin by your staying in a hotel or a continental pension (a fairly basic but usually comfortable lodging place, cheap but not usually providing meals) which should have been arranged for you. Do not leave the UK until you have satisfied yourself on this point.

### The limitations of hotel life

Unless your contract is destined to be short lived, you should start looking for a flat as soon as possible. Hotel life, although initially relaxing because of the lack of responsibility it offers, very soon becomes restricting because of noise, the physical confinement imposed by living in one room with a bathroom attached (remember you will be there at weekends as well), parking problems and the inconvenience of having to vacate or pay for your room every time you go home.

Taking a flat overseas may seem a big step but once established in their own premises, most contractors are very reluctant to contemplate returning to hotel life. Once again you must balance likely tenure against length of contract.

## Finding a flat

Seeking accommodation abroad is much the same as in the UK except for the language problem. Unless you speak the local tongue you will be forced to rely on the help of others. Flats to let are to be found in local newspaper advertisements and by enquiring in estate agents' offices. The latter do not always advertise their stock of premises to let.

Make sure that you understand the conditions of any lease that you sign and that you know exactly what your outgoings will be for services, etc. One month's rent in advance plus an equivalent, returnable deposit will normally be payable.

## Holiday flats

If the area in which you are working is popular with tourists, local people might have guest accommodation that they would be happy to rent to you. Ask at the local tourist office. If you arrive near the height of the season you may have to wait for the peak to pass before you can take possession. Be careful that there are no odd periods ahead for which the flat is already booked and which would entail your moving out. Generally speaking, you will not be required to sign a lease for holiday accommodation.

## A caveat

Finally, if you are seeking accommodation in Mediterranean lands, try and find a flat on the top floor. Southern continentals are fond of shouting, scraping furniture around and stamping about in wooden clogs on uncarpeted floors late at night. If this is happening on the floor above while you are trying to sleep, you might begin to wish you were elsewhere.

### Case history: discovering the true cost of accommodation

Alec Simons quickly learned that rented accommodation in Madrid was in short supply. When a flat did become available Alec was in competition with several other prospective tenants and took a calculated risk in signing the lease without having it translated first. He discovered after taking possession that a hefty charge was levied on all flats in the block for services and maintenance of the grounds and swimming pool. When he did have the lease translated, Alec further found that not only had he committed himself to renting the flat for a year but also to paying the full rent for that year whether he remained in the flat or not. He had assumed that if he left early, he would at worst lose his one month's deposit. As his contract was for a six month initial period, Alec could only hope that the likelihood of extension would become a reality.

## Question and answer session

Q.  *Is it worth considering unfurnished accommodation abroad?*

A.  Yes, but usually only where furnished accommodation is at a premium. Basic, second hand furniture can usually be obtained easily and fairly cheaply. This includes fridges and cookers, although unfurnished premises sometimes have these items built in. Furniture thus obtained can be sold, brought home or simply dumped at contract end. It can be quite surprising how little furniture is actually required for fairly comfortable living.

Q.  *If I rent a flat without a television, should I bring one out from home?*

A.  British televisions will need to be retuned to receive programmes abroad, unless you only want to watch videos. Conversely, if you buy a television abroad, it will need retuning for subsequent use in the UK.

## ARRIVING ON SITE

### First days on a UK contract

On UK contracts your first day on site will vary very little from starting a new job as a permanent employee. Having made your own way to the client's premises you will probably be taken to the personnel department for a standard introduction to the company and its procedures. If your work is defence related it is likely that you will be asked to sign security documents. Thereafter you will be shown to your place of work, introduced to your colleagues, shown the work that you are required to do and the rest is up to you. Apart from the natural strangeness of being in a new place and amongst different people, beginning a contract in the UK should present little difficulty.

**First days abroad**

It is when you work abroad that you will really feel the 'different-ness' of your situation. In most cases you will travel abroad on a Sunday and go straight to your lodgings rather than directly to your place of work. You will nearly always be met by somebody, either at the airport or at your lodgings, by the Team Leader, another contractor or a representative of the client company. This is an acknowledgement of the fact that you are a stranger in a foreign country and will require local assistance, particularly with the language.

The next morning you will be taken to the client's premises. You may well feel disorientated at this stage because of:

● tiredness from travelling

● unfamiliar surroundings

● a strange language

● disruption to your internal clock, i.e. European time is one hour ahead of UK time for much of the year and many Continental companies start work an hour earlier than at home.

Once you have been introduced to your new colleagues (including contractors if there are any there already), have satisfied the requirements of the local bureaucracy, e.g. registration with the local authorities where required (see Obtaining Residence and Work Permits, in Chapter 2), have been shown the whereabouts of such essentials as your office and desk, toilets, photocopiers, coffee machines and canteen you will probably be guided around the business end of the premises and then shown what is expected of you. Your first working day abroad will probably seem to pass very quickly and the sense of disorientation will quickly fade. Before long, you will hardly feel that you are abroad at all.

Whether you feel tense and anxious or confident and relaxed on your first day in a new contract, it is worth remembering that you are there for one reason—you are needed.

## SPOTLIGHTING THE TEAM LEADER

Some contract teams in the UK and most abroad, have somebody delegated by the agent to act as his representative on site. This is the Team Leader.

The position of Team Leader is often filled by a contractor known to the agent by previous association, or by the first on site of several contractors to be assigned to a particular client.

The responsibilities of the Team Leader vary from one contract to another but include:

● liaising with the client on personnel matters

● the collecting, signing and despatching of contract staff time sheets to the agent

● meeting new team members as they arrive on site

● arranging initial accommodation for new arrivals

● assisting with relations with the local bureaucracy

● keeping the agent informed as to future contract staff requirements

● sorting out problems in general.

On quiet, smooth running contracts being Team Leader can add interest as well as being mildly lucrative. On the rare, turbulent contract the position can be a trial.

### Question and answer session

Q. *Does the Team Leader have any responsibility for the work in hand?*

A. Not as a general rule. This is normally the preserve of the client and his own staff managers.

Q. *How is the Team Leader rewarded?*

A. On large contracts the Team Leader may have many contractors under his wing. The time he has to spend on their behalf is sometimes paid for jointly by agent and client for their mutual benefit. The Team Leader will receive his normal hourly rate for whatever professional function he fulfils plus remuneration for his extra duties. This latter payment may take the form of an addition to his rate or a monthly sum multiplied by the number of contractors in his care.

## CHECKLIST

1. Have you compiled a list of things to take with you?
2. Have you studied travel routes and obtained necessary maps and timetables?
3. Is your car in a fit condition for long journeys?
4. Do you have vehicle documentation for foreign travel?
5. Have arrangements been made for accommodation when you arrive on site?
6. Have you arranged medical and other insurances for working abroad?

# 5
# Life on Contract

There is far more to being on contract than simply coping with the job you have been sent to do. Unlike the man who returns from his permanent job to his own home every night and who can draw a line between job and home that divides his life into two distinct areas, you will as a contractor find that distinction far less clear.

## The contract outside the office
The environment in which you find yourself, the people you work and play with, the local population and your ability to co-exist with them, your accommodation and the frequency of your home visits are all interdependent elements of the overall contract situation. Your level of satisfaction with any of those elements can colour your attitude to the situation as a whole. Contractors sometimes leave their jobs because some aspect of the contract situation outside of their actual work becomes insupportable.

## Positive thinking
While some things, the people you work with for example, cannot be chosen, there is much that you can do to make your life on contract as amenable as possible. Merely recognising that you will have to make certain personal adaptations is a large step in the right direction.

This chapter has been designed to give you an idea of what life on contract is like and deals with:

- co-existing with other contractors, permanent staff and local people

- culture shock when abroad

- keeping yourself amused outside work

- having your family with you overseas

- coping with foreign languages

- home leave


## KEEPING A LOW PROFILE

Contracting, far more than in staff employment, is a question of survival. With the inevitable end of his contract hanging over him, the successful contractor is he who can delay that moment for as long as possible. This is achieved not merely by the efficient discharge of his professional duties but by keeping a low profile.

### Common sense

Keeping a low profile is largely a matter of common sense. Some contractors unfortunately, fail to recognise this and imagine incorrectly that the key to success lies in advertising their presence. The contractor who does not maintain a low profile is the one who:

- Makes noisy assertions about his expertise.

- Tries to push himself up the pecking order.

- Creates an image of himself that he may not be able to live up to.

- Makes the permanent staff feel inadequate and threatened by his presence.

- Upsets the locals, particularly when abroad and outside the workplace (small groups of Brits abroad are easily identifiable and word quickly gets back to the client company).

- Parades his assets before less well rewarded staff employees.

- Makes a disproportionate fuss over trivia to highlight his knowledge of his subject.


None of the foregoing will endear a contractor to the client, however productive he may be.

## The quiet route to success

The key to survival is quiet efficiency. This may not gain much notoriety but it is appreciated in the long run. One does not go on contract to seek promotion but to make money. The longer you can remain on a contract the better that purpose will be served. Some contractors stay long after the original purpose of their employment has expired simply by merging into the background and becoming accepted as a useful part of the furniture. Keeping a low profile may not do much for the ego but in the long run it pays.

## Case history: the perils of a high profile

Rob Dunhill was determined to make an impact from the moment he arrived on contract in Switzerland, his first abroad. He displayed his enthusiasm with eager and ceaseless discussion of the project, especially during lunch breaks which he spent with the client's management rather than with his contract colleagues. Sensing that he had made the right impression, he persuaded the client to allow him to work steadily increasing hours of overtime. Dunhill was soon working eighty four hours a week while other contractors were restricted to sixty hours, which in fact, was all that they wanted although that did not prevent resentment of Dunhill's special treatment.

Increasingly convinced of his indispensability to the project, Dunhill began to accrue to himself responsibility for its management, in which quasi-official capacity he spent most of his time submitting unsolicited reports on the progress of the job. When not so engaged he constantly pestered the agent for a rise in his hourly rate commensurate with his expanding role.

Eventually the client made an assessment of the performance of the contract team and its members and concluded that Dunhill's presence was adding nothing to the implementation of the project. When the team was reduced, Dunhill was one of the first to go, having promoted himself out of a job. Disbelieving, he stated that the client was making a big mistake in getting rid of its best people first.

Dunhill left Switzerland after only six months and apparently unaware, or refusing to comprehend, that if he had kept his mouth shut and his head down, he might have survived much longer. The contract actually lasted another five years.

## CO-EXISTING WITH YOUR COLLEAGUES

### Other contractors

You will make many friends on contract, hear their stories and share experiences. New horizons will open up as contractors compare notes and exchange agents' addresses. You will also learn a great deal about your own discipline if you are working with contractors from varied backgrounds, as you observe differing approaches to the job in hand.

### Close living

Because of the close existence that contractors lead, especially abroad where they may share the same hotel and socialise as well as work together, you will get to know your colleagues and their eccentricities very well indeed.

Contractors are often just that little bit larger than life, having some vital spark that distinguishes them from other mortals, if only for having made the break from the comparative normality of permanent employment. This can make them interesting, amusing or in some rare cases, insufferable.

However your fellow contractors strike you, be prepared for the need to be tolerant of them and their foibles. You may be together for a long time.

### Drinking with the boys

Needing company but lacking their own homes, families and friends around them, contractors socialise with each other and naturally gravitate towards pubs and bars at the end of the day. Often there is nowhere else to go. This is especially relevant abroad. As a result, many contractors tend to drink more than they would at home. Whilst this is not a problem for the majority, there are those who cannot keep their drinking under control and become a nuisance to themselves and those around them. Stories of famous drunks and their misdemeanours are rife in contract circles.

Go for a drink with the boys by all means but be ready to tell the man who wants to go on drinking all night that you've had enough (even if he hasn't).

### Permies

Once you become a contractor yourself you will encounter amongst other contractors an attitude of cheerful, professional disdain towards permies, or permanent staff employees. Permies are in fact, the breed against which contractors like to measure themselves, usually to the permies' disadvantage. This sentiment is sometimes reciprocated by a coolness amongst permies towards contractors, often based on an envious curiosity regarding the amounts of money that contractors are believed to earn, and about which contractors are unhelpfully and sometimes smugly tight-lipped.

Don't let this generic antipathy worry you; it is seldom expressed openly and very rarely sours the necessary symbiosis between contractors and permanent staff. Personal relationships also count for far more than tribal attachments.

### What's it like on contract?

Of one thing you may be absolutely certain. At some time you will be quizzed about contracting by the permies. Some will not rest in their efforts to find out how much you are earning. Others will hope to hear that contracting is a dreadful life fraught with insecurity and will probably go away believing that it was their own wisdom rather than lack of courage that has kept them permies all these years. A few will be genuinely interested in going contracting themselves and will be grateful for any tips you may feel inclined to pass on.

## LIVING WITH THE LOCALS

Apart from getting used to living away from home, contracting within the UK requires little or no adaptation, because you are operating in a culturally familiar environment.

### Adapting to conditions abroad

Contracting abroad is a different matter entirely. The greater the racial and cultural divide between yourself and your hosts, the greater the amount of adaptation and tolerance you will need.

However amusing, annoying, incomprehensible or illogical you may find the locals and their ways, the fact is that they are as they are and nothing is going to change them. It is you who will have to accommodate them.

At the very least, if you show respect for local customs it will be appreciated, even if you don't entirely understand them at first. If that respect develops into a genuine interest your hosts will be delighted.

The sooner you can traverse the cultural divide, the easier life will become.

## Avoiding splendid isolation

In the initial stages of a foreign contract you will naturally spend a high proportion of your free time with your fellow contractors, and perhaps with other British people who may be around.

The problem with this, at least in the long run, is that contractor communities abroad are seldom comprised of more than a few individuals and when they live closely together, soon discover the limitations of spending too much time with too few people. When you do not have enough variety in the company you keep, conversation becomes restricted, repetitive and eventually boring. The boredom itself can become a habit and the longer it endures, the more difficult it can be to break. It is very easy to fall into the trap of taking the line of least resistance, i.e. of socialising exclusively with your fellows simply because it is easier than making the effort of communicating with the locals, the very thing that can break the boredom.

The key to widening your circle of acquaintances, and to improving the quality of your life on contract abroad, is being able to speak to the locals in their own language (see below, Learning the Language). Although you will meet people who can speak English and will be happy to practise their skills on you, they will probably be in a minoriry.

## When isolation avoids you

There will inevitably be occasions when you will not have to seek out the locals because they will come looking for you.

One thing that many travellers discover abroad is how friendly people are. In some parts of the world you may find yourself overwhelmed with hospitality. Continental invitations can be very persistent and the polite excuse that might be acceptable at home may well fall on deaf ears abroad. Repeated refusals to accept hospitality will eventually offend your hosts no matter how many allowances they make for your Britishness.

This can be trying at moments when you may just want to be left alone to think your own English thoughts without having to struggle with a foreign language in an alien social environment. It is far better however, to acquiesce and where possible reciprocate. Being accepted by your hosts, even at the expense of a small sacrifice of your independence, is preferable to being rejected by them.

Co-existence is never easy and always requires a degree of effort to achieve. It is always worth expending that effort. Contracting abroad provides a wonderful opportunity to gain an insight into and understanding of other peoples and their ways and to appreciate a different viewpoint of the world.

Finally:

● remember that you are a guest
● don't isolate yourself from the host community
● be tolerant
● don't take the easy way out
● make the effort to communicate with the locals
● try to accept rather than to refuse invitations
● learn the language.

## LEARNING THE LANGUAGE

When contracting abroad you will inevitably encounter difficulties with the local language. Some contractors are content to muddle through, learning the bare minimum necessary for survival; others bluster with English and a few make a determined effort to converse with their hosts in their own tongue.

Each approach to the language problem has its merits according to circumstance. There is not much point in buying textbooks and attending courses if the contract is only likely to last two months. On the other hand if the job looks set to endure, it is a pity to waste the opportunity of learning another language in the environment in which it is spoken.

While it is true that some people have no aptitude for languages, at least in the academic sense, anybody can learn enough to facilitate communication. Your hosts, including the client company, will certainly appreciate the courtesy.

### Practical steps

At the very least, every contractor bound for a country where English is not the national or official language should take a phrase book and a dictionary with him. The more dedicated student will also require:

- a good grammar book
- a set of verb tables
- a textbook with written exercises.

A number of companies also market language courses using a combination of text and tape cassettes. Look for their advertisements in the Sunday papers or try any of the larger booksellers.

While home study is useful in learning a language, the best approach is to take a course in your host country. These are widely available in all major centres and even small villages will usually have somebody qualified to give lessons. Having an instructor of whom you can ask questions makes learning a language a lot easier than struggling on your own. In the unlikely event that you cannot find a course on your own, the personnel department of your client company may be able to help you.

Once you have achieved some competence in the local language and have begun to talk to people, you will find that life opens up and becomes much more interesting.

### Language as an aid to survival

All contracts come to an end. When the axe swings it is very seldom a case of dismissing everybody at the same time. The contract contingent is usually run down gradually and many factors come into play when the client is deciding who should go first. Personality counts as well as your particular function. Being able to speak the language not only enhances your usefulness to the project but helps to establish a rapport with the client. It could also help you to remain when others have gone.

### Long-term self-interest

Competence in foreign languages may also help you survive as a contractor. If an agent can tell a client in Hamburg that you are competent in German, your chances of being selected will be enhanced, although you probably won't be paid any more because of your ability.

## STAYING SANE ON CONTRACT

The title of this section might seem to suggest that contracting should carry a mental health warning.

Fortunately this is not the case. It should not be thought that when you go on contract you will be surrounded by people, of whom you will soon become one yourself, who exist permanently on the brink of a major breakdown. It is simply necessary to recognise that the contractor, notably abroad, is subject to pressures and reactions beyond those found in everyday staff employment. Recognising and coping with those pressures is part of successful contracting.

## The things that can get to you

It might be imagined that the greatest pressures would come at the beginning of a contract when one is subject to the double shock of leaving a permanent job and home simultaneously. Most people however, survive the transition unscathed and many actually find the challenge of their new situation stimulating.

The initial stages of a contract abroad, with the interest of a new job and the exploration of different surroundings, can seem like a glorious, paid holiday. The time enevitably comes though, when the novelty of both job and environment begins to wear off because:

● Working abroad does not mean that your job automatically becomes more interesting. Your working hours will be spent in an office much like any other, doing a job like any other.

● Even if you are lucky enough to be situated in a really interesting part of the world, you can remain a tourist for only so long. The most dedicated sightseer becomes tired of voyaging further every weekend in order to find something new and interesting.

This may be the point at which boredom sets in. Boredom is insidious and contagious, and can allow an unoccupied mind to dwell upon and magnify other negative aspects of the situation out of all proportion until they become actual pressures. Such include:

● isolation from family, friends and the home environment

● inability to communicate adequately

● close living with too few people

● frequent travelling between home and job and the need to readjust each time

- uncertainty in relating to a culture not your own

- frustration with the way the natives approach their work.

## Coping with the pressures

At home you always seem to have more things to do than there are hours in the day in which to do them, i.e. you don't have to look for ways to fill your time. On contract abroad you probably won't have any decorating or gardening to do so will have to look for ways to occupy your hours out of the office, other than by reading, watching television or sitting around in bars. This may require a determined effort because one of the nasty side effects of boredom is that the less you do, the less you want to do.

The trick therefore lies not so much in what you do to occupy yourself but in firstly recognising the need to do it and secondly, actually doing something about it. Ultimately, only you will know how best to occupy yourself profitably, but if you:

- have a transportable hobby, take it with you;
- play any kind of sport, look for it locally;
- wish to learn the language, sign up for classes.

Making the effort to fill your time as interestingly as possible is always worthwhile. It will keep boredom at bay and help keep other problems, if such there be, in their true perspective.

## TAKING THE FAMILY ABROAD WITH YOU

One of the distinguishing factors between the contractor and the permanent, non-contract employee who works abroad is that the contractor tends not to take his family with him. This is largely because of:

- *The unforseeable length of contract appointments*: the contractor, faced with a short initial period abroad and an indeterminate length of stay thereafter, will not usually consider it worth uprooting his wife and perhaps disrupting his childrens' education. It is easier for him to fly home for frequent long weekends and for his family to visit him abroad, perhaps during school holidays.

- *The type of accommodation that the contractor will choose*: if he is to make the most of his high income, he will wish to keep his foreign expenses to the minimum. This means that he will usually rent the smallest and cheapest accommodation that is compatible with a reasonably civilised existence. Whilst adequate for the single man, such accommodation will often be too small for the family as well, at least on a long-term basis.

## When the family comes too

Some contractors do of course, encourage their families to join them abroad. This tends to happen on contracts that have a long history behind them and a stable future before them. Other than the obvious benefits of family togetherness, the advantages can be:

- Excellent opportunities for wives and children to experience living abroad.

- Wives may find employment and children become bilingual through attending local schools for a sustained period.

- The man may find that his lady's presence actually improves his social life because women make contacts easily whereas a single male, past the age when most males are single, might be perceived as something of a predator and will find meeting people difficult. A couple is far more likely to receive social invitations than a lone man.

Some families become so entrenched that they begin to regard their foreign situation as home.

Such situations are in the minority, however, and entail hidden disadvantages such as:

- what to do with the family home in the UK. It can be risky to rent out the family house because of potential problems in regaining possession, perhaps at short notice should the contract terminate abruptly. It is also risky, for security reasons, to leave a house standing empty.

- The problem of boredom, which may afflict the contractor in time (see above, Staying Sane on Contract), can be far worse for his wife who may become dissatisfied with having little to do other than to relax and enjoy herself, however idyllic such an existence may sound. Unlike her partner she is unlikely even to have work to occupy her mind. Learning and speaking a new language will degenerate from fun to a chore and she will begin to yearn for her friends and activities back at home. In deciding whether to go home or stay she is facing the reverse of the dilemma that the contractor had to resolve before he left to work abroad.

## An assessment

Experience indicates that it takes about six months for a wife to reach the point when she feels that she wants to spend at least a prolongued holiday at home.

Contracting is essentially a bachelor existence. Marital harmony and overall practicality are generally better served by the family remaining at home with frequent visits from the bread winner and the occasional family trip abroad.

## Question and answer session

Q. *My wife would like to join me if I go on contract abroad. Will she need a residence permit?*

A. If you need a residence permit, so will your wife if she remains for longer than the permitted 'holiday' or 'tourist' period (frequently about three months) of the country concerned. Contact the relevant embassy, consulate or High Commission. A visa may also be required.

Q. *Will my wife be able to work when she joins me?*

A. Within the EU she has the same right to work as yourself with no work permit required. The further you go outside the EU, the more difficult it can be for accompanying wives to work. Some third world countries expressly forbid it.

Q. *What precautions should we take if we decide to rent our house out?*

A. You must

- noticy your accountant because there may be an income tax liability

- consult your building society in case changes need to be made to your mortgage agreement/insurance policy

- appoint an agent to handle the actual letting, preferably a member of the Association of Residential Letting Agents or somebody other appointed by yourself

- advise your house structure/contents insurers

- draw up a proper tenancy agreement

- inform the police.

Q. *What should we do about schooling abroad?*
A. Local schools can be used in the West but if the language of instruction is not English, or if your child is at a critical stage in his/her education, you may be obliged to find and pay for private, British style education. In less developed parts of the world, expensive private education may be the only option.


## SEX, MARRIAGE AND THE CONTRACTOR

More contractors get divorced than married. Although this may be a reflection of the current, high divorce rate, it is also a comment on a life style because:

- No married man can tell what effect his going away from home on contract will have on his domestic situation until he has actually gone. However minutely a couple may discuss the pros and cons of the breadwinner leaving home to go on contract, it is the unforseen consequences of that departure that can bring relationships to grief.

- Sometimes it is the mere strain of separation that proves unendurable. In other cases the couple simply grow apart while occasionally the partners in a marriage find that they enjoy their new liberty so much that they decide to make it permanent. Sometimes the freedom for either partner to enter into new relationships becomes irresistible.

There is no easy answer to the problem. Sometimes it is no problem at all. Some contract marriages actually thrive on separation, absence truly making the heart grow fonder.

## Contracting is a team effort

However you and your partner resolve the matter of your being away, the one who remains at home will have as much coping and adapting to do as the one who goes. For the married contractor, a wife who can stay behind and run his home for him, taking on the burden of many of the things that her absent husband would normally do, is as much a contributor to the successful outcome of the contract as the contractor himself. She too earns the rate.

## IS BRITISH REALLY BEST?

Quite apart from the necessity to adapt to your host country's social conventions when contracting abroad, a further requirement for tolerance exists in the workplace where national characteristics may present a different organisational approach to work even though technically the job may be the same as at home.

## How to confuse a contractor

Such differences frequently lead to much puzzlement among British contractors. They will shake their heads at the apparent chaos around them and wonder how the locals ever manage to achieve anything. You will often hear contractors comment that they thought British industry was bad enough but 'out here' it's even worse. Their next observations may well be that:

● Everything that you hear about foreign industry being efficient is rubbish.

● The foreign worker is less diligent and productive than his British counterpart.

● If the managers employed abroad were to try their hand in the UK their true worth would be exposed and they wouldn't last five minutes.

● If industrial efficiency and personal endeavour were true criteria, then British industry should dominate the world.

The fact that it doesn't and that many of these incompetent, disorganised foreigners enjoy a better standard of living then we do only compounds the puzzle.

## The surprise of the unexpected

In making these observations and being mystified by them, the contractor is experiencing a mild dose of culture shock. No matter how long he works abroad, he is likely to remain perpetually bemused by, for example:

- *Germans*, famed for their efficiency and thorough planning, who seem to fix their eyes on a point on the horizon and blunder clumsily towards it creating confusion in all directions until the project founders and devolves into a series of noisy meetings that result in the whole job having to be started afresh.

- *Italians*, who seem quite incapable of making calm, individual decisions, much preferring to labour the minutest detail en masse with much arm waving and senseless noise when nobody can possibly hear what is being said anyway.

- *Swiss*, infuriatingly dogmatic and blinkered of vision, who appear to operate in little, independent cells that never communicate with each other and issue endless, contradictory directives.

- *Spaniards*, forever avoiding committing themselves to anything and leaving everything to the last minute when there will be a mad scramble to get the job done.

- etc., etc.

Because he is a foreigner with a unique viewpoint and his own ways, the British contractor notices these national characteristics and perceives them as weaknesses. Sometimes, if he allows himself to dwell too long upon them, they can become the only thing that he sees.

## A rationalisation

The fact of the matter is that others have their own ways of doing things. The job gets done in the end and probably won't have taken any longer than it would at home. The route leading from concept to completion simply follows different paths in different places. A foreigner working in British industry might be tempted to throw up his hands in horror at the way we do things, or in his view, don't do them.

As a contractor assigned to a foreign company you will encounter unfamiliar ways of approaching a job. You may even conclude that the British way is better and that the foreigners have a lot to learn. You could well be right. They might even be glad to benefit from your expertise. At the same time they have managed quite nicely until now so they can't be all wrong. British is quite often best. Sometimes somebody else is even better.


## GOING ON LEAVE

Unlike the permanent employee working overseas, whose terms of engagement will probably specify the length and frequency of his paid leaves, the contractor is fortunate in that he can take leave more or less when he wants to as long as the client company agrees to his absence. He will not of course, be paid while he is away from work.

### Weekending in the UK

Most contractors working in Britain stay within feasible motoring distance of home, leave work early on a Friday and drive back during Monday morning. Client companies generally appreciate that contractors often live a long way from the site and are tolerant of their working less hours on Mondays and Fridays and more for the rest of the week.

If you will be working in the UK but too far away to drive home at weekends, you will have to use public transport and this will often entail flying which means that weekend journeys must be planned in advance (see Travelling but Mostly Flying, in Chapter 4).

### Taking leave from overseas

As in the UK, foreign companies accept the need for contractors to work somewhat irregular hours owing to the requirement to travel to and spent time at home. It would be an unreasonable company that made it difficult for you to take long weekends in the UK at regular intervals.

Contracts situated close to home, in the Netherlands for example, mean that short, frequent leaves are possible in terms of cost and time spent travelling.

Further afield in Europe, leaves are generally longer and taken less frequently as cost and journey time increase. Contractors needing to make expensive, intercontinental journeys often restrict their visits home to one or two long leaves per year. Those without domestic commitments usually travel home less frequently than the family man regardless of their work location.

### Spacing out leaves

In general, contractors in Europe tend to work for three of four weeks at a time and then take a long weekend at home, often flying out on a Thursday afternoon and back on a Monday to return to work on the Tuesday. Time lost is made up during the weeks before the next leave.

Where longer leaves are concerned, during the summer break for instance, many contractors spend all or part of their holidays abroad in order to preserve the one sixth.

### Planning a break

When planning leaves from abroad, take the following into account:

- Book flights sufficiently in advance to take advantage of cheap rate air tickets.

- Avoid travelling during British or foreign public holidays when public transport can become horribly crowded and subject to delay. This can usually be achieved by going one day before or after the main rush. If you are coming home for Easter for example, it is preferable to travel early on Good Friday morning rather than attempt the journey the day before when the whole of Europe is on the move. The day's work that you have gained on the Thursday stands you in credit to return one day later and thus miss the rush again.

- Buy your tickets abroad (see above, Travelling but Mostly Flying). The local travel bureau will be able to tell you the peak periods and how far ahead of them you should book. Very few British travel agents will have any knowledge of foreign public holidays and other special local conditions.

● Always take the one sixth into account.

## Case history: less often, less exhausting

In his early days as a contractor, Neil Crowhurst used to try and come home from the Netherlands every weekend. He soon found though, that there were disadvantages to this. The first was the obvious one of the cost of air fares. The second and less obvious disadvantage was that his time at home, severely limited by the one sixth, meant that no sooner had he arrived than it was time to go back again. Such time as he was able to spend at home was difficult to enjoy because of tiredness from travelling.

Eventually Neil decided that longer, less frequent weekends at home were more enjoyable. He also saved on air fares and found returning to work less of a trial than following immediately after two closely spaced journeys as formerly.

## Question and answer session

Q. *Do I discuss leaves and holidays with the agent, before contract signing for example?*

A. As a rule, no. The agent will nearly always say that leaves are a matter to be arranged between yourself and the client. Client interviews can be a good opportunity to gently mention and test reaction to your anticipated leave schedule.

Q. *Who pays my travel costs when I go on leave?*

A. You do, always. Only at the beginning and the end of an assignment does the agent provide travel expenses.

Q. *Do I have to take major holidays at the same time as the client's staff?*

A. This varies according to company, country and pressure of work. Some firms in southern Europe shut down completely during August and may expect you to take leave then. Be prepared to be flexible.

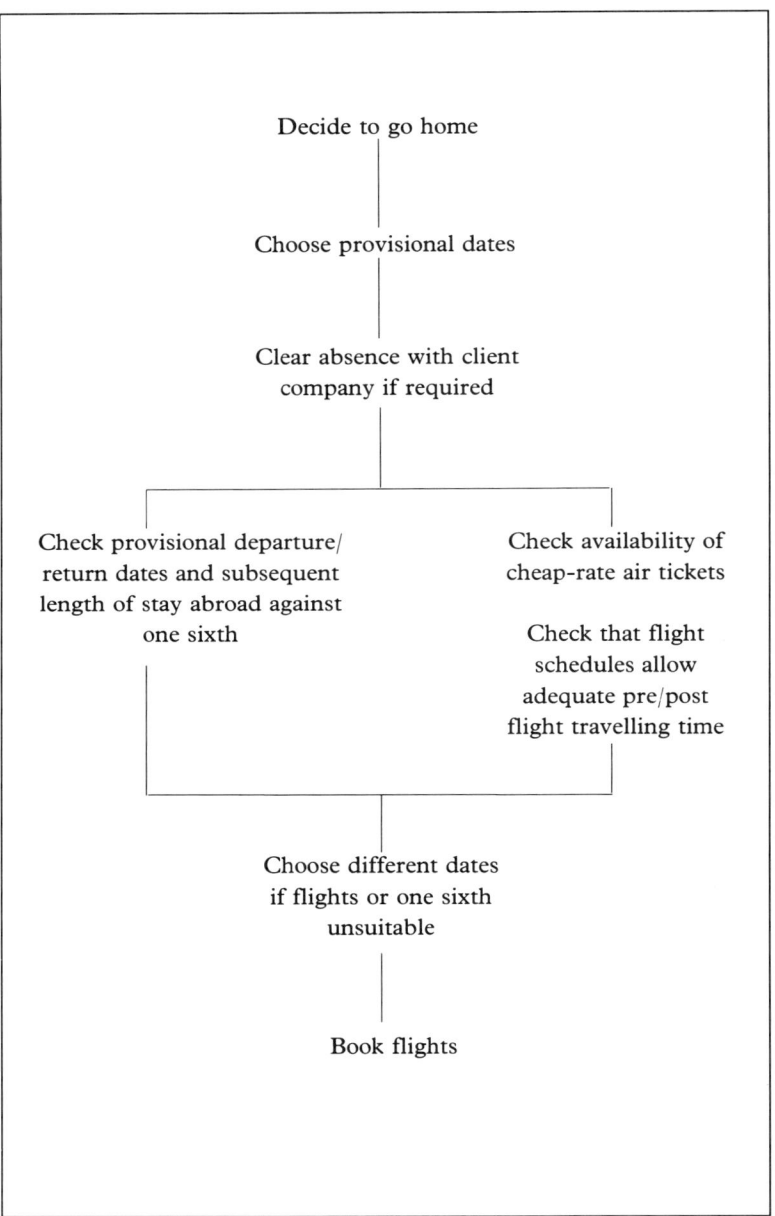

Fig. 16. Planning home leave.

## CHECKLIST

1. Have you obtained language books if you are bound abroad?
2. Do you have any hobbies that you can take abroad with you?
3. Are you prepared to lead a bachelor existence abroad?
4. Have you considered the One Sixth Rule when planning leaves from abroad?

# 6
# Looking Ahead

## MAINTAINING CONTINUITY

Maintaining continuity of employment is of supreme importance to the contractor. A long period without an income can negate all the advantages of having become a contractor in the first place. The only contractor who can afford to rest on his laurels is he who has generated some financial independence.

### When a contract ends
All contracts come to an end eventually, because either:

- the project concludes, or
- the contractor decides to move on.

Unexpected crises notwithstanding, very few contracts end suddenly. Even before notices are issued there will be plenty of signs that the end is approaching, even if that end is still several months away. The signs can be:

- work begins to run down
- the project may be approaching completion
- overtime is reduced or stopped
- the rumour machine begins to hum.

When the contract contingent is reduced you may not be the first to go and even if you are, you will still have a notice period during which you may find another contract.

### Finding another contract
Locating a second and subsequent contract is much the same as finding your first one, except that you now have the major advantage of contract experience behind you, both professionally

and in dealing with agents. You are also a more marketable commodity to an agent than somebody who is coming fresh from permanent employment with no contract experience at all.

Whether your departure from a contract is voluntary or enforced, use the period before the end to find yourself another assignment, as follows:

- Update your CV to reflect your latest experience.

- Talk to your current agent. He will have a good idea of the status of your present contract and will be anxious to replace the income that he is about to lose when his contract team is run down, although it is fairly unlikely that the agent for whom you have been working will have another job for you immediately. A change of contract usually means a change of agents.

- Telephone and send CVs to as many agents as possible, including those who may be currently advertising and those whose details you have been adding to your contact book. (*See* Fig. 17) Even if an advertisement is a year or more old, it is quite possible that the project for which a particular vacancy was advertised is still running and might need staff even though no new announcements have come to your notice.

- Include a covering letter with your CV.

### The value of personal contacts
Personal contacts count for as much in contracting as in other fields. This can be particularly true when you are looking for a contract because:

- Other contractors may tip you about current or forthcoming openings.

- Agents with whom you have a good relationship may consider you before they advertise or search their files.

- Fellow contractors may be asked by their agent if they know anybody suitable for a particular vacancy.

- Companies for whom you have previously worked, and

32 Evington Crescent
Mellingbury
Bristol BS99 9XZ
28 March 199X

Mr K. Simons
Techexperts Ltd
Avarice Row
London WC21 4XY

Dear Mr Simons

Please find enclosed my current CV. My present contract in Germany is due to terminate shortly and I shall be available for a further assignment in the UK or overseas.

I can be reached on 01049-890-0000 (office; probably until the end of April), or on 01272 00000 (home number; messages forwarded). I look forward to hearing from you.

Yours sincerely

Christopher J. Thompson

Fig. 17. Letter of enquiry to agent at end of contract.

perhaps with whose key staff you have established a good relationship, may ask for you by name.

## Question and answer session

Q. *If I wish to leave a contract because I want a change, will my present agent help me?*

A. Probably not. As far as he is concerned you are a known quantity earning money for him. Even if he could find another position for you, he will then have to replace you in your present position with attendant disruption to his client's project.

Q. *If my present contract ends before I have found another, should I worry?*

A. Not necessarily. The minute you become free, your chances of finding work are greatly enhanced simply because you are immediately available. It is also much easier to talk to agents from the comfort of your own home than it is to make and receive surreptitious phone calls from your place of work.

## TURNING YOUR HAT ROUND

One of the great advantages of contracting is that it presents more opportunities to step sideways into a different and perhaps more lucrative discipline than is usually the case in permanent employment.

This can happen because:

● An agent may be unable to find suitable people to fill a particular requirement and will search his files for contractors with skills in an allied or similar field. If agent and client are agreed that the situation warrants taking a calculated risk and the contractor feels sufficiently confident that he can handle the new discipline, everything may work out to the benefit of all concerned.

● As one stage of a contract runs down and new ones begin, a client may move an existing contractor, known to be reliable and adaptable, from one function to another rather than bring in a fresh man who is an unknown quantity.

It is always worth asking, as your own assignment approaches its end, whether the client could use your services in another capacity. You have after all, absolutely nothing to lose.

Some contractors thus remain on one project for years, moving between disciplines and gaining valuable experience, emerging at the end of the contract with a quite different and more marketable job title.

### Turning a problem into an opportunity

Finally, should you arrive on a contract and find that the job you are required to do is quite different from what you had been lead to expect, don't despair. If the job interests you and you think that it is within your capabilities, the client may agree to give you the time to learn. You have the advantage that you are already there. If you can make a favourale impression on the client he may calculate that you are a better risk than somebody totally unknown to him, assuming that the agent can even find a suitable person ready to start work at the drop of a hat.

Whilst you should never wilfully talk yourself into a job for which you are totally unsuited, never dismiss the idea of trying something new.

## HOW LONG DO I STAY A CONTRACTOR?

The average person usually has an attainable objective in mind when he breaks into contracting; paying off the mortgage is the most commonly cited example.

Few contractors though, actually give up contracting once they have achieved their objective. This is because:

● contracting as a way of life becomes a habit
● it is difficult to give up a contract income
● being a contractor can change your outlook fundamentally.

### Expanding horizons

As the mental habits of permanent employment fade they are replaced by fresh perspectives of the world gained through working in a contract ambient, perhaps with other contractors who may have established incomes from their investments and who may be looking forward to early retirement (at least from working for other people). You will naturally wonder whether you could do likewise.

Redeeming the mortgage can suddenly seem a very limited ambition. Surely, you will tell yourself, it is worth spending a few more years on contract to achieve some greater end. It is often at this point that some greater, long-term objective begins to emerge.

## When the contracting has to stop

A contractor is rather like the old prospector, heading into the wilds with his mule on one last search for gold. But like the prospector, the contractor comes to realise that he will have to call it a day sometime.

Three factors, together or separately, can contribute to a decision to quit:

- wanting to, e.g. tired of a nomadic existence
- needing to, e.g. domestic pressures
- being able to, e.g. rich enough to give it up.

Whenever the end comes, be it by accident or design, it is part of successful contracting to be ready for it rather than to be caught out by it. This means accumulating as much capital as you can as quickly as you can. You will be helped in this if you:

- Never consider contracting as an end in itself, but as a means to an end.

- Never regard a contract income purely as increased spending money.

- Never allow your expenses to rise to the level of your contract income.

- Never make any financial commitment that can only be serviced by a contract income.

- Never put yourself in a financial position that will cause you anxiety regarding:
  —the continuance of your current contract
  —the availability of subsequent contracts.

  *Caution:* More than a few contractors ignore the above to their eventual regret, regarding a contract income as a bottomless crock of gold. When the time comes to quit they are unable to, and are forced to remain on the circuit when they are past their own contract 'sell-by' date.

However you plan to live in your post-contract era, make sure that you get the best advice you can at an early stage. This will help you to remain a contractor only for as long as you want to and not for as long as you need to, and may free you from the necessity ever to return to staff employment (see below, Going Permy).

### Case history: a gentle withdrawal from contracting

After Dave Morgan had been contracting for a few years, he came to realise that he would probably never be quite rich enough to retire on the interest earned by his investments. While he had no intention of remaining a globe-trotting contractor forever, he had no wish to return to the restrictive environment of staff employment either. Contracting had given him a taste for freedom that he found agreeable and wished to perpetuate. His own business seemed to provide the answer.

Over the years, Dave had seen several of his colleagues suddenly give up contracting, commit their savings to business ventures that had failed and had been forced back into contracting as a result. Dave decided to implement his exit from contracting more slowly, developing his passion for boat building into a full time business over a period of years. By supporting it initially out of his contract income and by subcontracting most of the actual manufacturing, Dave was able to continue contracting until the business became self-financing. Gradually he found that he was spending more time with his boats than he was on contract, until the point was reached when the business became fully viable and Dave no longer needed to go contracting.

## GOING PERMY

The idea of eventually returning to permanent employment may be the furthest thing from your mind when you are signing your first contract. Most contractors though, have to face the prospect of seeking permanent staff employment at some time or other. This can happen when:

- there is a gap in contract opportunities

- the contractor feels that he should spend some time at home

- he is tempted by his contract client with the offer of a staff position

- he finally gives up contracting.

## Once a contractor . . .

Whatever the need, the notion of returning to staff employment is anathema to most contractors. This is revealed in the saying 'once a contractor, always a contractor', often quoted by the afflicted with a mixture of pride and a tacit acknowledgement of having succumbed to the addiction that contracting can become.

Contracting is not just a matter of making money but also one of personal development. The case-hardened contractor, with diverse service at home and abroad behind him, is not the same person who originally and wonderingly went out into the world. His experiences will have broadened his horizons and his personality will have expanded to fill the roles required of him.

## The problems of going permy

The contractor who returns to permanent employment can find it as difficult as becoming a contractor in the first place because he may:

- Experience difficulty in relating to staff colleagues who lack his perspectives, have no breadth of vision or spirit of adventure.

- Experience a reverse culture shock upon his return to British industry if he has been abroad, finding it moth-eaten, stuffy and hierarchical with poor working conditions.

- Feel that he is taking a backward step, not just financially but also in personal terms.

- Feel trapped and long to be back amongst others who think as he does.

- Eventually start phoning around the agents and looking at the small ads again.

Certainly you will meet contractors who have tried going permy and found that it did not satisfy their souls. They return to contracting and remain there even when they would sooner be at home, rather than re-live the permy experience.

## Additional problems

The contractor who genuinely wants to go permy may face problems in even obtaining a staff position. Having been a contractor in however elevated a role or discipline, is not necessarily a recommendation and can arouse jealousy in prospective employers and their representatives if they suspect that you are better off than they are.

An interviewer may interpret your contract experience with its possible, frequent changes of location as a sign of your instability and therefore unsuitability for employment. He may suspect, however unjustly, that you only intend staying until you find another contract. Even if he believes that your intentions are honourable, he may have had dealings with other, equally sincere ex-contractors who, after a short period of permanent employment, have given in to their addiction and gone back on the contract circuit. He might even be a former contractor himself, fidgeting to be free.

## Avoiding going permy

The moral to the story is to avoid returning to staff employment if you possibly can; the experience of the majority of those who have tried it suggest that you will not like it. If you can identify a long-term objective as early in your contracting career as possible, you may never have to consider going permy again.

## Question and answer session

Q.  *My client has told me that my contract will end soon but that I am welcome to transfer to his permanent staff. What should I do?*

A.  Your client has paid you a compliment because he obviously values and wishes to retain your services. If you want to go permy, then do so, but remember your present agency contract will almost certainly state that you may not accept employment with the client without the agency's prior written consent. If you don't want to go permy and are prepared to seek another contract, thank the client for his offer and tell him that you are only prepared to remain as a contractor. He may well reconsider.

*Q. Should I close down my limited company if I go permy?*

A. Not immediately. You may need it again because the chances are that you will not remain a permy very long. It costs money to wind up and then re-establish a company.

## CHECKLIST

1. Don't wait until your present contract is over before you start looking for another.
2. Is your CV updated and ready to send out?
3. Have you kept your contact book up-to-date?
4. Are you prepared to try a new discipline?
5. Have you considered your long-term future?

# Conclusion

## Should I be doing this?

When you find yourself worrying about the future as you contemplate going on contract, you are no different from the vast majority of established contractors who were once permanent staff employees themselves. Each had to make the conscious decision to become a contractor. Each probably worried about how he would cope with leaving the security of a staff job and living and working away from home, possibly in a foreign country. It was no easier for him than it will be for you. It is natural and indeed healthy to wonder if you are doing the right thing. Only the most insensitive of people barge into contracting without due consideration and they are often the ones who run into trouble.

## Will I succeed?

Nobody can guarantee success to the would-be contractor but similarly, there is absolutely no reason why he should not succeed as long as he has perseverance, endeavour and the wit to avoid the traps that ensnare the unwary, the brash and the careless.

Contracting may seem to be fraught with hazards and in some respects it is. All however, are avoidable. There is no inevitability to each and every contractor ending up as a high paid refugee dodging from one project to the next, pursued by ex-wives and creditors, hounded by the tax man, living on alcohol and tranquillizers and keeping one jump ahead of mental disintegration. A few do come to grief, it is true, but they are in the minority and are often the authors of their own misfortunes.

## Will contracting change me?

Contracting will change you in the long run. As a contractor you will move around more than most people. Every new situation will leave its mark upon you, your persona constantly being moulded by the imposition of each new experience upon the last. After several years of expanded experience you may find it difficult to subsequently narrow your horizons. Even visiting an airport may have you looking at the destination board and wondering what contracts lie just a plane ride away.

## Will it achieve anything?

Treated carefully, contracting will enable you to greatly improve your financial position and achieve objectives otherwise quite unattainable. If you are determined and circumspect there is no reason why in the future, with several contracts behind you, you should not be comfortably off and in a position to do as you want with your own life. You may even meet ex-colleagues from your last staff employment, still doing the same old job, in the same old place for the same inadequate money, and wishing they had taken the plunge and gone contracting too.

# Further Reading

*Contract Documentation for Contractors*, Smith, Powell & Sims (BSP Professional, 0 632 02275 2, £25.00)

*Contracting your Services*, Davidson, (Wiley, 0 471 50694 X, £22.65)

*Contractors Training Staff, Guide for*, Engineering Industrial Training Board D4, (Engineering Industrial Training Board, 0 85083 707 3, £1.00)

*Contracts of Employment, Making and Varying of*, Leighton & Doyle (Polytechnic of London, 0 946232 067, £1.00)

*Contracting and Subcontracting for Overseas Projects*, Hadley & Herzfeld, (Graham, Trotman, 1 85333 025 6, £25.00)

*Contract Documentation for Contractors*, Smith, Powell & Sims, (BSP Professional, 0 632 02275, £25.00)

*How to Write a CV That Works*, Paul McGee, (How To Books, 1995)

*Introduction to Contractors All Risk Insurance*, Eaglestone, (Books, Books, Books, 1 85452 061 X, £12.95)

*The Job's Yours*, Waddington (Paper Fronts; Elliott Right Way Books, 0 7160 0853 X, £2.50)

*Obtaining Visas and Work Permits*, Roger Jones, (How To Books, 1996)

*Succeed at Your Job Interview*, Heavyside, (BBC Business Matters, 0 563 36742 3, £5.99)

*Working Abroad: Essential Financial Planning for Expatriates and Their Employers*, Golding (International Venture Handbooks, 1 85876 007 0, £15.00)

*Working Abroad: You and Tax*, Oliffe & Greaves (Deloitte, Haskins & Sells, 0 86349 127 8, £5.95)

*Working Abroad: Daily Telegraph Guide to Working and Living Overseas*, Stewart & Golzen (Kogan Page, 0 7494 01680, £8.99)

*Working Abroad: Tax Implications of*, Chortoc Books (1 85355 056 6, £8.00)

# Appendix 1
## Secretaries/Administrators of District Societies of Chartered Accountants

(Information supplied by the Institute of Chartered Accountants.)
The following may be contacted to assist you in locating an accountant in your area:

*Beds, Bucks & Herts*: Mrs W. J. Clark, 22–36 Hastings Street, Luton, Beds. LU1 5BE. Tel: (01582) 31600.

*Birmingham & West Midlands*: Mr M. A. Robinson FCA, Stock Exchange Building, 33 Great Charles Street, Queensway, Birmingham B3 3JH. Tel: (0121) 236 5832 or 5741.

*Croydon & District*: Mrs A. V. King JP, 5 Jordan Close, Sanderstead, South Croydon, Surrey CR2 0JW. Tel: (0181) 651 0420.

*East Anglia*: Mr C. P. D. Walmsley FCA, St Andrews Castle, 33 St. Andrews Street South, Bury St. Edmunds, Suffolk IP33 3PH. Tel: (01284) 750469.

*Humberside*: Mr P. S. Milne MA, 49 Salmon Grove, Hull HU6 7SZ. Tel: (01482) 466400.

*Leics. & Northants*: Mr K. N. Woodthorpe FCA, 4th Floor, York House, 91 Granby Street, Leicester LE1 6EA. Tel (0116) 551491.

*Liverpool*: Mr J. H. H. Mounsey FCA, Second Floor, 1 Old Hall Street, Liverpool L3 9HG. Tel: (0151) 236 2401.

*London*: Mr B. J. M. Edmunds FCA, ACMA, Friendly House, 52 Tabernacle Street, London EC2A 4NB. Tel: (0171) 490 4390.

*Manchester*: Mr P. G. D. Holden BSc, FCA, Derby House, 12/16 Booth Street, Manchester M2 4AL. Tel: (0161) 832 4281.

*North West*: Mr R. Strahan, 55 Garstand Road, Preston PR1 1LB, Tel: (01772) 53950.

*North*: Mr J. L. Hinkley FCA, 6 Market Street, Newcastle-upon-Tyne NE1 6JF. Tel: (0191) 232 8815.

*Nottingham*: Miss A. M. Jepson FCA, Grosvenor Chambers, 23 King Street, Nottingham NG1 2AY. Tel: (0115) 412286.

*Sheffield*: Mr M. J. W. Venning FCA, 2a Rutland Park, Sheffield S10 2PD. Tel: (0114) 681450.

*South East*: Mrs H. C. Brook BA, SESCA, Bridge Gate, 55–57 High Street, Redhill, Surrey RH1 1RX. Tel: (0137) 768601.

*South Essex*: Mrs P. E. Wilkes MBIM, 46a Crossways, Shenfield, Brentwood, Essex CM15 8QY. Tel: (01277) 220052.

*South Wales*: Mr P. Fletcher MISM, 129 Cathedral Road, Cardiff CF1 9UY. Tel: (01222) 220972.

*South West*: Mr J. W. E. White FCA, c/o Green Acre, Court Road, Newton Ferrers, Near Plymouth, Devon PL8 1DD. Tel: (01752) 673567.

*South*: Mr A. J. French MBIM, Fryers, Norley Wood, Lymington, Hants SO41 5RR. Tel: (01590) 65297.

*Staffs, Salop & Wolverhampton*: Mr G. Fielding ACA, 5th Floor, Stock Exchange Building, 33 Great Charles Street, Queensway, Birmingham B3 3JH. Tel: (0121) 236 5832/5471; (01902) 23033.

*Thames Valley*: Mr J. C. Sprent, 16 College Avenue, Maidenhead, Berks SL6 6AX. Tel: (01628) 34146/28610.

*West*: Mr E. R. Avery, Dartington & Co Ltd., 70 Prince Street, Bristol BS1 4QD. Tel: (0117) 213206.

*West Yorks*: Mr R. C. M. Webb BA, FCA, 27 Park Square, Leeds LS1 2PL. Tel: (0113) 456475/442044.

See also: The Institute of Chartered Accountants in England and Wales *Directory of Firms* (ISBN 0 333 54312 2), published by Macmillan. This publication has over 12,000 entries listing practices in the UK and overseas with their names, addresses, telephone and fax numbers and specialisations. This publication is priced at £50 to non-members of the Institute, so consult the reference section of your local library.

(See also Appendix III.)

# Appendix 2:
## Agents/Recruitment Specialists/ Consulting Engineers Specialising in Engineering Related Contract Appointments

*Note:* Whilst the following information is believed to be correct at the time of publication, complete accuracy cannot be guaranteed.

Other addresses may be obtained in the pages of the publications listed in Appendix III. Software and IT engineers should consult the *Freelance Informer*.

Ablative Ltd., Little Mead, Kenn, Clevedon, Bristol, Avon BS21 6ST. Tel: (0117) 343584.

Apex Technical Services Ltd., 300 Hotwells Rd, Hotwells, Bristol, Avon BS8 4NW. Tel: (0117) 277612.

Aquinas Ltd., 117 Two Mile Hill Rd, Kingswood, Bristol, Avon BS15 1BH. Tel: (0117) 613535.

Assistance Teknica Ltd., York House, Borough Rd., Middlesborough, Cleveland TS1 2HJ. Tel: (01642) 224545.

Author Services (Technical) Ltd., 4 Ichnield Way, Letchworth, Herts. SG6 1EX. Tel: (01462) 481144.

BDSL Ltd., Park House, Greenhill Crescent, Watford, Herts. WD1 8QU. Tel: (01923) 229234.

Beechwood Recruitment Ltd., Beechwood Appointments Register, 221 High St., London W3 9BY. Tel: (0181) 992 5658.

BePOS (Bechtel Personnel & Operational Services Ltd.), PO Box 1413, Broadway Chambers, Hammersmith Broadway, London W6 7PW. Tel: (0181) 846 6910.

BJ Consultants Ltd., Austen House, 1 Upper St., Fleet, Hants. GU13 9PE. Tel: (01252) 622202.

Butler Service Group (UK) Ltd., King's Mill, King's Mill Lane, South Nutfield, Surrey RH1 5NE. Tel: (01737) 822000.

Calco Services, Lawrence House, 9 Woodside Green, London SE25 5EY. Tel: (0181) 655 1600.

Capital Labour Harlow Ltd., 4 Market House, The High, Harlow, Essex CM20 1BL. Tel: (01279) 431025.

CG Consultants Ltd., Clearglen House, 151 Frimley Rd, Camberley, Surrey GU15 2PS. Tel: (01276) 682733.

Cliveden Technical Recruitment, Tudor Building, 161–163 Bittern Road, Southampton, Hants. SO18 1BH. Tel: (01703) 229094.

Contec Services Ltd., 819 Bath Rd, Bristol, Avon BS4 5NT. Tel: (0117) 717688.

Datasource Computer Employment Ltd., 3 Imperial Square, Cheltenham, Glos. GL50 1QB. Tel: (01242) 521358.

DATA Contract Personnel Ltd., 114 Bridge St, Warrington, Cheshire WA1 2RU. Tel: (01925) 573336.

DBM Technical Services Ltd., 39 Main Ave, Moor Park, Northwood, Middx HA6 2LH. Tel: (01923) 821622.

DBM Scotland Ltd., 7 South Gyle, Broadway, Edinburgh, Scotland EH12 9ED. Tel: (0131) 316 4088.

*Note:* The above two companies are unconnected.

Deekay Technical Recruitment Ltd., 2 Davyhulme Circle, Urmston, Manchester M31 1SS. Tel: (0161) 747 1234.

DTG Ltd., 1a Leaphill Rd, Boscombe, Bournemouth, Dorset BH7 6LS. Tel: (01202) 417725.

Elgood Technical Personnel Ltd., 2 The Hide Market, West St, St Philips, Bristol BS2 0YK. Tel: (0117) 414000.

EPC Ltd., Orchard Chambers, 189a London Rd, Reading, Berks RG1 3NU. Tel: (01734) 661222.

EPP Ltd., 168 Cheltenham Rd, Bristol, Avon BS6 5RE. Tel: (0117) 425093.

Essential Personnel Ltd., 10 Frogmore, High Wycombe, Bucks HP13 5DG. Tel: (01494) 462646.

Expertwise Ltd., The Annexe, Century House, High St, Hartley Witney, Hants RG27 8NY. Tel: (01252) 844991.

GECI International, Kingsgate Business Centre, 12–50 Kingston Road, Kingston on Thames, Surrey KT2 5AA. Tel: (0181) 541 1877.

Ferrari Offshore Ltd., Hussar Court, Westside View, Waterlooville, Hants. PO7 7SE. Tel: (01705) 230511.

Grafton Technology Ltd., Mitre Court, 16 Commercial Rd, Parkstone, Poole, Dorset BH14 0JW. Tel: (01202) 740750.

Graphic Engineering Design Ltd., Church House, Church Rd, Filton, Bristol, Avon BS12 7DD. Tel: (0117) 792396.

Hartley Services Ltd., 46 Victoria St, Manchester M3 1ST. Tel: (0161) 839 0305.

Howard Organisation Ltd., Recruitment and Resourcing Division, Crompton Rd, Stevenage, Herts SG1 2EE. Tel: (01438) 746600.

H & M Engineering Projects, 821 Bath Road, Bristol, Avon BS4 5NT. Tel: (0117) 776670.

HS Consultants Ltd., 131 High St, Codicote, Herts. SG4 8UB. Tel: (01428) 821400.

IBPI Engineering Ltd., Dale House, 204 London Rd, Hazel Grove, Stockport, Cheshire SK7 4DF. Tel: (0161) 419 9020.

Ian Marshall Staff Recruitment Ltd., 11 Great Russell St, London WC1B 3NH. Tel: (0171) 255 1696.

In-Line Ltd., Bishops Weald House, 2–14 Worthing Rd, Horsham, West Sussex RH12 1SL. Tel: (01403) 262345.

Intec Recruitment Ltd., 41 High St, Frimley, Surrey GU16 5HJ. Tel: (01276) 691345.

Ingineur Ltd., Pendicke St, Southam, Warks. CV33 0PN. Tel: (01926) 817612.

Intereurope Technical Services Ltd., Unit 6, 6 Wedgewood Way, Stevenage, Herts. SG1 4QB. Tel: (01438) 745777.

IVM Engineering Derby Ltd., Challenge House, Suite 15C, Sherwood Drive, Bletchley, Milton Keynes MK3 6DP. Tel: (01908) 643645.

Ligvale/UTS Ltd., The Walk, High St, Billericay, Essex CM12 9YB. Tel: (01227) 868135.

Link Technical Services Ltd., 60 Borough Rd, Middlesborough, Cleveland TS1 2JH. Tel: (01642) 246155.

Loftminster Ltd., Bowmaker House, 134 Borough Rd, Middlesborough, Cleveland TS21 2ES. Tel: (01642) 223218.

Mascotech Engineering – Europe Ltd., Canewdon House, Locks Hill, Rochford, Southend-on-Sea, Essex SS4 1BB. Tel: (01702) 541581.

Marchtech Engineering Ltd., 1631 Solent Business Park, Southampton PO15 7AH. Tel: (01489) 575883.

MGT (Technical Services) Ltd., Suite 206, Lombard House, Croydon, Surrey CR4 3JP. Tel: (0181) 665 6680.

Morson International Ltd., Stableford Hall, Monton, Eccles, Manchester M30 8AP. Tel: (0161) 707 1516.

OMI Logistics Ltd., 75 The Esplanade, Weymouth, Dorset DT4 7AA. Tel: (01305) 783472.

Parkway Designs, The Birchcliffe Centre, Hebden Bridge, West Yorks HX7 8DG. Tel: (01422) 845569.

Pipers Ltd., 153 High St, Rayleigh, Essex SS6 7QZ. Tel: (01268) 775599.

Project Engineering Consultants (UK) Ltd., 1 High St, London Colney, Herts AL2 1RE. Tel: (01727) 821818.

Pipco Ltd., 8 Stuart Rd, High Wycombe, Bucks. HP13 6AG. Tel: (01494) 459333.

Real-Time Consultants plc., 118–120 Warwick St, Royal Leamington Spa, Warks. CV32 4QY. Tel: (01926) 313133.

Ricardo Aerospace Ltd., Brunswick House, Upper York St, Bristol BS2 8QN. Tel: (0117) 9240088.

Shoreline Engineering Recruitment Ltd., 14a East St, Portsmouth, Hants. PO9 1AQ. Tel: (01705) 473515.

Shorterm Engineers, 31 Yorktown Rd, Sandhurst, Camberley, Surrey GU17 8DX. Tel: (01252) 878512.

Staffhire Ltd., 3 St Mary's Courtyard, Church St, Ware, Herts SG12 9EG. Tel: (01920) 460461.

Strongfield International plc., 62 Marylebone High St, London W1M 3AF. Tel: (0171) 224 1200.

STS Recruitment Ltd., Unit 1, Crown Walk, Jewry St, Winchester SO23 8RY. Tel: (01962) 869478.

TAP Engineering Ltd., 81a Marylebone High St, London W1M 3DE. Tel: (0171) 935 2668.

Technical and Engineering Services Ltd., Central Chambers, The Broadway, Ealing, London W5 2NR. Tel: (0181) 579 6360.

Technical Aid International Inc., Star Lane House, Staple Gardens, Winchester, Hants. SO23 8SR. Tel: (01962) 877777.

Technical Manpower (UK) Ltd., PO Box 1268, London W4 2JA. Tel: (0181) 995 4747.

Technology Project Services (International) Ltd., Mill Studio Business Centre, Crane Mead, Ware, Herts SG12 9PY. Tel: (01920) 487148.

Techskill UK Ltd., Suite 17, Venture House, 5th Ave, Letchworth Business Park, Letchworth, Herts. SG6 2HW. Tel: (01462) 682282.

WA Consultants, General Accident Building, Greenway Rd, Torquay, Devon TQ1 4QB. Tel: (01803) 315334.

Woodland Consultancy Services, Sun Alliance House, 29 Bromley Rd, Kent BR1 1DG. Tel: (0181) 464 7524.

# Appendix 3:
## Associations/Publications

The associations/publications in the following list are orientated more towards 'working overseas' than to contracting and this is reflected in their Sits. Vac. columns, but their journals contain articles whose subject matter may be relevant to the overseas contractor. The exception is the 'Freelance Informer' which caters especially for the contractor in software and information technology.

The journals are useful sources, through their advertisements, of names and addresses of organisations supplying support services for contractors, i.e. limited company formation, accountancy, insurance, networking, etc.

*Freelance Informer*, Reed Business Publications Ltd., Quadrant House, The Quadrant, Sutton, Surrey 5MT 5AS. Tel: (0181) 652 3500. Journal: *Freelance Informer*, weekly, sub. £40 p.a. (£90 p.a. o/seas).

Expatriates Association, Court Mill Lane, Court St, Trowbridge, Wilts. BA14 8BR. Tel: (01225) 753643. Journal: *The Expatriate*, monthly, £1.75.

Overseas Jobs Express, PO Box 22, Brighton, Sussex BN1 6HX. Tel: (01273) 440220. Journal: *Overseas Jobs Express*, Fortnightly, sub. £16, 3 months.

Expat Network, International House, 500 Purley Way, Croydon, Surrey CR0 4NZ. Tel: (0181) 760 5100. Journal: *Nexus*, monthly, sub. £25, 3 months.

# Glossary

**Accounts.** Record of income and expenditure.

**Aduana.** Spanish Customs post.

**Apex/Super Apex.** Cheap rate travel ticket bought at least two weeks in advance of flight or journey.

**Agent/agency.** Organisation specialising in the recruitment of contract staff for placement with client companies to meet specific expertise/manpower shortages.

**Assignment.** The project/contract to which a contractor is assigned.

**Aufenthaltserlaubnis.** German residence permit, obtainable from the Rathaus (town hall).

**Autobahn.** German motorway

**Autopista.** Spanish motorway

**Autoroute.** French motorway

**Autostrada.** Italian motorway

**Availability.** A measurement of the contractor's freedom to accept an assignment, e.g. immediate; period of notice from present job; to termination of current assignment.

**Bureau de change.** Internationally used French term for currency exchange.

**Carte de sejour.** French residence permit, issued by the Mairie or Prefecture.

**Cambio.** Italian/Spanish currency exchange

**Carta di soggiorno.** Italian residence permit, obtainable from the Questura or Caribinieri.

**Certificate of Incorporation.** Certificate issued by Companies House, Cardiff confirming incorporation of limited company. Copy usually required by agency at contract signing where contractor is operating as limited company.

**Certificate of Third Party Liability Insurance.** Certificate (where issued, if not the policy) of Contractor's limited company third party liability insurance, usually to £1,000,000. Copy usually required by agency at contract signing where contractor is operating as limited company.

**Charge rate.** The rate that an agency charges a client for a contractor's services, i.e. the contractor's rate plus the agency's percentage.

**Client.** The agency's customer, usually a company or other organisation, to whom a contractor is assigned.

**Corporation tax.** The tax payable on a company's annual profit.

**Contact Book.** Contractor's expanded address book containing agency addresses, phone numbers and details of contract possibilities.

**Contractor.** Individual assigned by an agency to a client to provide specific expertise or service.

**Contract documentation.** The actual contract agreed between and signed by agent and contractor, defining the nature of an assignment and its terms and conditions, plus other relevant documents.

**Cowboy agent.** Sharp operator prepared to use unethical, if not downright illegal business practices, especially in his dealings with his own contract staff.

**CV.** Contractor or aspiring contractor's abbreviated but comprehensive employment/achievement record (formerly called résumé).

**Database.** Any computer based store of information, in this case an agency's file of contractors and their names, addresses, disciplines and personal details, used to match individuals with customer requirements.

**Discipline.** The trade, skill or profession practised by a contractor within an industry or field.

**Dogana.** Italian Customs

**Douanes.** French Customs post.

**DSS.** Department of Social Security.

**Duration.** The length of time that a contract is expected to last initially/lasts eventually.

**EU** The European Union, formerly the European Community and consisting of Austria, Belgium, Denmark, Finland, France, Germany, Greece, Ireland, Italy, Luxembourg, Netherlands, Portugal, Spain, Sweden, UK.

**Eurocheque.** Cheques issued in booklets of ten, supported by a plastic card and encashable in all European countries plus some in north Africa and the Middle East, in the currency of that country or other currency if required.

**Exchange rate.** The prevailing value of one currency against another. Details to be found in most daily newspapers or any bank.

**Flughafen.** German airport

**Green Card.** Internationally recognised document confirming the extension of insurance cover for a motor vehicle for use in countries other than its country of origin.

**Gendarmerie.** The police in France and other French speaking countries.

**Host country.** The foreign country in which a contract assignment is based.

**Income tax.** Tax payable on an individual's personal income.

**Initial period.** The period of time, stated on the contract documentation, for which a contractor is assigned to a client. The eventual length of the assignment may be much longer.

**International driving licence.** Document issued by the Automobile Association containing details of the holder's driving licence, translation into many languages, photograph of holder. Internationally recognised.

**Interview.** Meeting between an agent and/or client and a contractor, to determine the suitability of the contractor for a particular project (and the attractiveness of the client, his project and premises to the contractor).

**Invoice.** Weekly/monthly statement submitted to agent by contractor's limited company of payment due by agent for services rendered by contractor to client company. Invoice to be accompanied by timesheet signed by client.

**Lease.** Document signed by lessee and lessor defining property to be leased and terms and conditions pertaining to lease, in the context of this book, a flat or other dwelling rented to a contractor for a specific period.

**Limited company.** Company limited by shares and registered with Companies House, Cardiff. Contractors are increasingly required to operate as limited companies.

**Location.** The actual place in which a contract assignment is situated.

**Networking.** Expression used to describe the system whereby a contractor utilises the services of a 'shell' company based offshore as an alternative to establishing his own limited company.

**NIC.** National Insurance Contributions.

**Objectionable clause.** Any clause in a contract document deemed unacceptable by the contractor and/or his solicitor.

**Offshore company.** A limited company established by the contractor outside the British mainland and commonly in the Channel Isles, Isle of Man or Eire.

**Péage.** French motorway toll.

**Peaje.** Spanish motorway toll.

**Period of notice.** Period of time to be worked between resignation from staff position or contract and date of termination of services.

**Registration.** The act of recording one's residence in a foreign country with the civil authorities.

**Rate.** The contractor's hourly or less commonly, daily rate of pay for his services to a client, quoted in Pounds for UK contracts and in Pounds or in local currency as applicable for foreign overseas contracts.

**Residence permit.** Official sanction granted by a foreign country for a contractor to live in that country.

**Self employment.** In this context meaning that the contractor is self employed and not operating either as a PAYE employee of the agent or through his own limited company.

**PAYE.** Pay As You Earn, i.e. income tax is deducted at source by employer, as in the case of a staff employee or contractor employed directly by agency instead of through contractor's limited company.

**Permanent staff.** Permanent employee(s) of company, not contractor, 'Permy' in contract parlance.

**One sixth rule.** The rule that enables contractors working abroad to avoid UK income tax on their earnings as long as they spend no more than 62 days per year in the UK on a rolling one sixth basis over 365 days.

**Reciprocal agreements.** Agreements between the UK and foreign governments regarding the application of taxation and social security rules to their citizens when working/residing outside their national territories.

**Security clearance.** Clearance required by the Ministry of Defence for people working in projects with a national security element e.g. defence equipment.

**Team Leader.** Member of contract team, usually abroad, appointed by agent to represent his interests and handle administrative matters.

**Travellers cheques.** Cheques issued by bank in Sterling or other currency, paid for at time of purchase and encashable overseas.

**VAT.** Value Added Tax, applicable at different rates throughout the EU and administered in the UK by HM Customs and Excise. Threshold for registration (1994/95), turnover of £47,000 p.a.

**VAT Certificate.** Certificate of registration for VAT of individual, his business or limited company, issued by local VAT office. Copy normally required by agency at contract signing for VAT registered contractors.

**Vignette.** Swiss motorway pass.

**Visa.** Sanction granted (normally as stamp in passport) permitting holder to visit or work/reside in foreign country; usually issued initially by embassy, consulate or high commission of that country in the UK and sometimes renewable within the country concerned. Some countries will not let holders leave until they have obtained exit visas.

**Visa card.** Internationally recognised card issued by holder's bank. Used to pay for goods and services and to obtain cash. Charged to the account number shown on the card.

**Wechsel.** German currency exchange.

**Work permit.** Sanction granted permitting holder to visit or work in foreign country; usually issued initially by embassy, consulate or high commission of that country in the UK and sometimes renewable within the country concerned. May be stamp in passport and/or additional documentation.

**Zoll.** German Customs post.

# Index

159